Podcasting
and Blogging
with **GarageBand** and **iWeb**

Podcasting
and Blogging
with **GarageBand** and iWeb

Robin Williams and **John Tollett**

 Peachpit Press • Berkeley • California

Podcasting and Blogging with GarageBand and iWeb
Robin Williams and John Tollett

Published in association with SpiderWorks Press
www.SpiderWorks.com

Peachpit Press
1249 Eighth Street
Berkeley, California 94710
800.283.9444
510.524.2178
510.524.2221 fax

Find us on the web at **www.Peachpit.com**
To report errors, please send a note to errata@peachpit.com
Peachpit Press is a division of Pearson Education

Copyright ©2007 Robin Williams and John Tollett

All original illustrations, art, and design
    ©2007 John Tollett and Robin Williams

Interior design by Robin Williams
Interior production by Robin Williams and John Tollett
Index by Robin Williams
Editing by Dave Mark
Prepress by David Van Ness

ISBN
0-321-49217-X

10 9 8 7 6 5 4 3 2 1

Printed and bound in the United States of America

Contents

7   Add your Podcast to the iWeb Site   101

The Index

Podcasting
and
Blogging
with
GarageBand
and
iWeb

This book is dedicated to Robin's mom,
the intrepid Pat Williams,
who is probably the only 77-year-old woman in the world
with her own podcast that she made herself!
And she learned to do it using this book.

:-)

What is Podcasting & Blogging Anyway?

A **blog** is a personal journal, posted on a web page for anyone to read.

A **podcast** is, essentially, an audio blog; you can listen to a podcast on a web page, in iTunes, or download it to an iPod. Some podcasts include video, but it is much easier and often just as effective to create an audio blog and include still images.

The following pages explain in detail what blogs and podcasts are and show a number of examples of the way some of our friends are using iWeb and GarageBand to post their creations.

What You Need

This book assumes you have three things:

1. A Macintosh computer.

2. The iWeb and GarageBand software. These are both included in the Apple software package called *iLife '06* (or later). If you bought a new Mac recently, *iLife* might already be installed.

   You'll use iWeb to create a web site to hold your blog and podcast, and you'll use GarageBand to create your podcast.

3. A .Mac account. This account costs $99 a year, but the perks it comes with are invaluable. There is no easier way to post web sites, blogs, and podcasts, plus there are so many other benefits. Just go to Apple.com, click the ".Mac" tab, and either sign up for an account or get a free sixty-day trial.

What is a Blog?

A **blog** can be like a diary that's available on the Internet for anyone to read, or it can be a source of valuable information in your area of expertise. Blogs can range from a minute-by-minute update on a developing news story to yearly updates on Grandma's pet cat—and everything in-between.

Blogs are often just forms of personal expression, places to rant, complain, observe, ponder, criticize, honor, praise, preach, report, or ramble. A blog can provide important information to a class, business associates, family members, or any other group.

Blogs have become a very important means of disseminating information, as well as developing a community among like-minded hearts and souls.

The ease and immediacy of blogging has made it a popular and useful phenomenon. If you can type, you can blog.

Why create a blog?

There are probably almost as many reasons to blog as there are blogs. Some blogs are outlets for self-expression and creative writing, while some are centered around discussions of social and political issues, news, technology, and anything else you can think of. Many of the most popular blogs are informative and offer instruction or guidance.

Blogs you create in iWeb can include a feature that allows you to receive comments from readers. This can add another level of communication to a blog—family, friends, or associates can use the blog as a communication tool rather than just a one-sided newsletter.

A blog can help organizations publicize themselves and keep current information available either for the public or for select personnel. The head of a company, church, school, or any other type of organization can maintain a constant dialog with associates, students, and other interested parties.

If you have something to say (or think you do), blogging is for you.

What is a Podcast?

A **podcast** is an *audio* blog—you listen to it rather than read it. It's like having your own radio show that everyone around the world can tune in to whenever they want, not just at the moment you happen to be recording or broadcasting. Podcast *episodes* are placed on a website, where people can *subscribe* to them. Subscribers are automatically notified when a new episode is available—by the podcast player software installed on their computers (iTunes for Mac users). But listeners don't have to subscribe to a podcast to listen to it; anyone with access to the podcast's web address can go there and listen.

Listening to episodes on your computer isn't the only way to enjoy podcasts. One of the biggest attractions of podcasts is that they're portable. Anyone with an iPod (or some other MP3 player), can transfer episodes from a computer to their player and listen when and where it's convenient—in the car, while grocery shopping, at the gym. This is how an increasing number of people stay updated with their favorite news, sports, and entertainment sources.

Most podcasts are simply audio files. It's easy, however, to create *enhanced* podcasts that include graphics, photos, and even web page links. As you'll learn in Chapter 6, it's easy to create an enhanced podcast, placing photos or graphics in a timeline so they appear precisely when you want them to appear.

Video podcasts are also popular. They're as easy to make as audio podcasts if you have a video camera and know the basics of editing video in iMovie (see Chapter 10). A video podcast (also know as a **vlog** or **video blog**) is a movie file that's been compressed and resized (smaller) to a format that's compatible with the web.

Video podcast files are much larger than audio podcast files. They take up more room on your web site's storage space and they use more bandwidth when viewers watch them. If your podcast gets too many viewers, your web host provider may charge you extra for bandwidth usage.

Why create a podcast?

Podcasts will become as ubiquitous as web sites and blogs as people realize how useful they are. For instance, one podcast that you'll see examples of throughout this book allows members of the Mary Sidney Society around the world to participate in monthly luncheons that are held in Santa Fe, New Mexico. They can listen, at their convenience, to podcasts of the presentations. Members can even create their own podcasts so we can play them at the luncheons or broadcast them on the society site.

Examples

On the following pages are a few live examples of blogs created by people using iWeb, as well as podcasts by people using GarageBand and iWeb.

Community pages

Robin's mother, Pat Williams, heading towards 80 years old, maintains a blog and podcast for the retirement community in which she lives. She creates it all on her Mac, and even though many of the other retirees use PCs, they can listen to and enjoy her reportings of the goings-on in the community.

Pat volunteers for the Yountville visitor center (say hello when you stop in) and posts web pages of events. Thank goodness for the Mac— it keeps her off the streets.

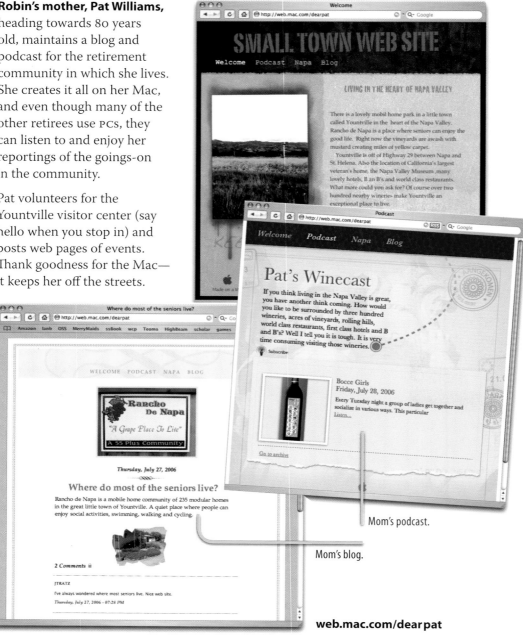

Mom's podcast.

Mom's blog.

web.mac.com/dearpat

6

Entertainment

Clayton Lobaugh is an enterprising young teen who, sometimes with the assistance of his friend Antonio Marquez, channels a lot of energy into making hilarious video podcasts (see Chapter 10 for tips on making video podcasts). As Clayton says, "Podcasting is a brilliant way of creatively using self-expression. I'm having a ball making these podcasts, but the main reason I am doing these is in the hopes of making people laugh because most people need to lighten up. If someone sees my site and cracks a smile at the antics of that 'crazy red-haired kid,' then my work here is done . . . not literally, of course. (In my podcasts, any resemblance to persons living or dead is 'purely coincidental')."

web.mac.com/claytonfunnyguy

Clayton creates video podcasts.

Professional use

Marketer **Louise Roach** and web designer **Hope Kiah** formed the Web Marketing Mavens as a vehicle to share their skills in search engine optimization (SEO).

They teach workshops in web marketing for beginners, and on their site they offer a web marketing blog and a free podcast about marketing.

When planning their web marketing, Hope and Louise knew they needed a carefully optimized site built in a high-end web design application. But they created their

www.WebMarketingMavens.com

web.mac.com/webmarketingmavens

podcasts with Garageband, iWeb, and a .Mac account and linked their main web site to the .Mac podcast—and vice versa. The iWeb site closely matches the original site design so visitors won't even notice they changed servers.

Their "recording studio" is an echo-absorbing walk-in closet, complete with clothing! Hope added the podcast to the iTunes Music Store directory where it can be found by typing "podcast on marketing."

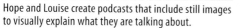
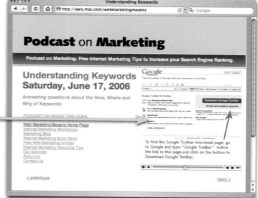

Hope and Louise create podcasts that include still images to visually explain what they are talking about.

Journals of all sorts

Denise Kusel is a journalist who's taking off on a road trip across the country. She plans to spend time in campgrounds talking with people about what's happening in our country and how they feel about their lives. Along the way, she'll be using her cell phone to connect to the Internet and her iWeb site to blog and podcast her stories. Her blogs include comment links so readers who follow across the country can also share their stories with her.

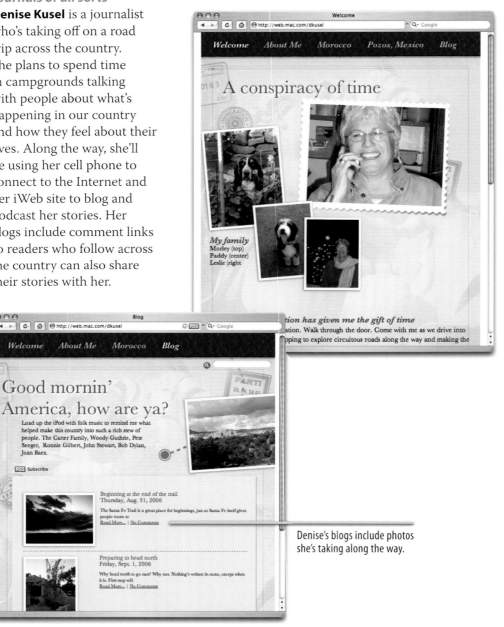

Denise's blogs include photos she's taking along the way.

web.mac.com/dkusel

Broadcasts of meetings

The **Mary Sidney Society** has a monthly luncheon series with a twenty-minute presentation at each meeting. So that members around the world can "attend" the luncheons, we podcast the presentations. And if someone from outside Santa Fe wishes to do a presentation, they can send us a podcast and we can use that as our presentation at a meeting. The world is getting smaller all the time!

web.mac.com/marysidney

These podcasts will include photos from the presentations.

Companion sites to other projects

John Tollett wrote a great little book, *Macs on the Go,* about traveling with your Mac laptop and getting connected anywhere in the world. John can even get connected in a phone booth in Cameroon.

What would have been a daunting task—to develop a special companion web site for a book—became a half-day job using iWeb and GarageBand.

iWeb makes it easy (and fun) for him to update information and to add podcasts and other interesting items, such as tips, blogs, and anecdotes.

The site also makes it easy for other Road Warriors to contact him and add their own mobile adventures.

web.mac.com/roadrat

John's blogs include great tips for mobile computing.

Finding Published Blogs and Podcasts

There are millions of blogs and podcasts out there. Fortunately, finding one that interests you is not as daunting as it might seem. Every day, new blog and podcast directories are being published, some of them quite specialized. For instance, **BlogHer.org** focuses on blogs by women (or men who are writing about women's concerns). **Technorati.com** ranks sites in order of popularity based on how many links go to a particular blog site.

Use a directory

In your browser, search for "podcast directory" or "blog directory" and you'll come up with many sites that categorize podcasts and blogs. Either browse through their lists of sites or use their search feature to find a blog or podcast on a particular subject.

If you find a directory you like, you can even submit your blog or podcast to them (find their "Submit" or "Add your Podcast" button; see Chapter 9).

Use iTunes to find podcasts of interest

iTunes has a directory of podcasts that have been submitted to and approved by Apple. An advantage to using iTunes to find podcasts is that you can immediately listen to them and even subscribe to them through a program you are familiar with, and you can easily download them to your iPod, just as you would music.

One way to find the directory in iTunes

1   Open iTunes.

2   In the Source pane on the left side of iTunes, click on "Music Store," as shown below.

3   In the genre pop-up menu, circled below, choose "Podcasts." Now you can search, browse, narrow down the categories, etc.

Another way to find the directory in iTunes

1 Open iTunes.

2 In the Source pane on the left side of iTunes, click on "Podcasts," as shown below.

3 This not only displays a list of the podcasts you have subscribed to, but there is also a link to the directory in iTunes, circled below. It takes you directly to the screen shown on the previous page.

An Overview of the Blog Process

Before you begin, here is what you can expect to do to get your blog created in iWeb and posted to a web site hosted on your .Mac account. We assume you've got the Apple software *iLife '06* and a .Mac account* (as explained on page 3).

1 Open iWeb and create a "Welcome" page. You can do this in less than five minutes.

2 Add a "Blog" page.

3 Use the "Entries" page to create a new blog entry. Edit the page, edit the text, add photos, etc.

4 Click the "Publish" button.

5 View your site on the web!

An Overview of the Podcast Process

Before you begin, here is what you can expect to do to get your podcast created in GarageBand, added to your iWeb site, and posted to your .Mac account. We assume you've got the Apple software *iLife '06* and a .Mac account* (as explained on page 3).

1 Open GarageBand and talk to your computer to record your podcast.

2 Edit your podcast, if you like—add or delete audio, add photos, music, chapter markers.

3 Choose the Share menu to "Send Podcast to iWeb."

4 Edit your podcast "Entries" page in iWeb.

5 Create at least a "Welcome" page in addition to the podcast page (if you don't already have one).

6 Click the "Publish" button.

7 View your site with its podcast on the web!

8 Submit to iTunes with a few clicks of the mouse.

*Alternatively, you can post the site on your own server,
  as explained in Chapter 8.

Build an iWeb Site!

Now that you're ready to blog, we'll first show you how to build an iWeb site because your blog will go on this site.

If you want to skip straight to podcasting, first build your Welcome page (see the following page) and become familiar with editing the template, then jump to Chapter 4.

Be sure to spend the time to create and customize your Welcome page, following the instructions in this chapter. Then, when you add your blog and podcast pages, you will already feel comfortable with making the necessary modifications.

These are the steps you'll go through to set up your site:

1 Create a Welcome page.

2 Edit the text and graphics.

3 Click the button to publish it to your .Mac account.

You can build more than one web site in iWeb. Each site can have its own collection of pages and will have its own web address. But all of them will always appear in iWeb every time you open it; that is, you don't open one site in iWeb and work on it, then close that site and open the other—whenever you open iWeb, every site you have created will be available in the main window.

Start Building your Web Site

You'll be amazed at how easy this is. Just follow these simple steps to **create a Welcome page** as the basis for your site:

1 Open iWeb. Then choose one of the following:

If this is the first time you have opened iWeb, go to Step 2.

If you already have a site that you want to add to, make sure you have a Welcome page in it. If you do, skip to the next page. If you need to add the Welcome page, click the plus button at the bottom-left of the iWeb screen, then go to Step 2.

If you already have a site and you want to add a second one, go to the File menu and choose "New Site." Then go to Step 2.

If you already have a site but you want to get rid of it, first start your new site: Go to the File menu and choose "New Site." Then go to Step 2. Later you can delete the site you don't want; see page 32.

2 In the "sheet" that drops down from the title bar (shown below), scroll through the template samples on the left side. Single-click on one of the template masters on the left to display its page variations on the right.

3 In the right-hand pane, double-click on the "Welcome" page. The sheet will disappear and a Welcome page will appear on your screen, ready for you to edit, as shown on the following page.

If you don't create a Welcome page that is the first item in the list of pages, your web address will be long and dreadful!

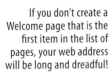

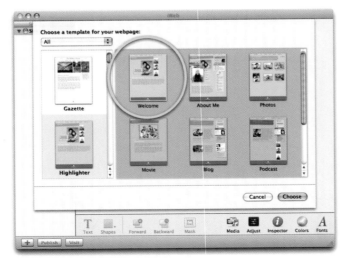

Customize your pages

Your page contains placeholder text and images. Notice that in the "Site Organizer" on the left side of the iWeb window, the Welcome page is selected. When you add more pages, you'll use this Site Organizer to select the ones you want to display and work on.

Replace placeholder text

Double-click on any text to select it, then type your own text.

Replace placeholder images

You can replace all the images on the page. If you've been storing your photos in iPhoto, use the Media Browser to easily replace the existing images:

1 Single-click the Media button at the bottom of the iWeb window.

2 Single-click the "Photos" tab.

3 All of your images in iPhoto are available here. Just find the image you want and drag it on top of one of the existing photos in the template.

Or drag an image from anywhere on your hard disk and drop it on any photo on this page.

This is the Welcome page template from the "Highlighter" master, before modifications.

Most elements on a page can be moved, resized, or deleted.

Customize the text

Not only can you replace the actual text with your own words, you can change the font, the style, the size, and the color, just as you've always done in a word processor.

1 Simply select the text (double-click a word or press-and-drag over a selection).

2 Click the "Fonts" button to open the list of fonts.

3 Choose a "Family" of fonts, then a "Typeface," then the "Size."

4 To change the color of the text, either click the color box in the Font palette, or click the "Colors" icon in the iWeb toolbar.

If you like to really fine-tune your type, use the Type pane of the Inspector, as shown on page 30. Using the Type Inspector, you can change the alignment (left, right, center), adjust the spacing between individual characters, between lines of type, and between paragraphs. You can also change the color of the background of the paragraph, and adjust the placement of the text in its box (at the top, centered in the middle, or at the bottom).

One way to change the color of text is to click this box to open the Colors palette.

This text is selected and ready for you to edit or change its properties.

To open the font preview, drag this tiny dot downward.

Customize the graphics

You can resize, rotate, and move images. The placeholder photos in iWeb are automatically placed inside a "mask," which crops the photo to fit inside. You can adjust the cropping, or take it out of the mask altogether. First, let's work within the mask.

To select the photo beneath the mask, double-click on it. You'll see a shaded-back area that indicates the portion of the photo that is not visible, as shown below. (If you double-click and don't see the shaded area, it means the image fits neatly into the space.)

There are eight of these handles on a *selected* image. If you don't see these handles, the image is not selected.

After you double-click on a photo, the pointer turns into the hand cursor when positioned over the image.

To move the image around inside the masked area (this will change the cropping of the photo), *press* in the middle of it with the hand cursor and drag.

To resize the image, position the tip of the pointer on any handle (the little white square on each corner and side) and drag. The image will resize in proportion as you drag.

To resize the image from the middle (instead of from the handle on which you dragged, as above), hold down the Option key and drag any handle.

To rotate the image, hold down the Command key. When you position the pointer over a handle, it turns into a curved arrow. Keep the Command key down and drag a handle to rotate.

Use the Graphic Inspector

Select an image or graphic object and then open the Graphic pane of the Inspector. Experiment with the options: add a graphical border, a drop shadow, or a reflection; make the image see-through (lower the "Opacity").

Click this button to open the Inspector, then click on the Graphic icon, as shown to the right.

In the example above, we dragged a photo onto the page. In the Graphic Inspector, shown to the left, we applied a graphical border to it, chose the color and the width of the border (5 points), and applied a reflection.

We clicked on the Text tool (the T) to create a text block, typed the word, gave it a "color fill" of blue, and added a thin border of dots. We used the "Forward" button to bring it in front of the photo.

Add a photo to a page

You can add photos or other images to the page without putting them in the masks that are in the template. Just drag an image from the Media Browser or from anywhere on your hard disk and drop it anywhere on the page.

Add a mask

To add a mask to an independent image, just select it and click the "Mask" button in the bottom toolbar. Once you have applied a mask, you can double-click on the image inside and move it around inside the mask to crop it.

To delete a mask, select the image and click the "Unmask" button in the toolbar across the bottom of the window. If the button says "Mask" instead of "Unmask," that means there is no mask on the *selected* image.

Name the Site and its Pages

The Site Organizer pane lists all the pages and sites you create. Yes, you can build and post more than one web site (from the File menu, choose "New Site"). iWeb provides generic default names for the sites and all the pages, but you can change them, as explained below.

It's especially important to rename your pages if you plan to have more than one site and each site will have its own blog and/or podcast, as you'll see later.

Rename the pages

We renamed the Welcome page to "Home."

To rename a page, double-click it in the Site Organizer (shown to the left) and type a new name. Page names are used as links in the navigation bar at the top of every page. It's best to use short names to prevent the navigation bar from becoming crowded. It's also best to avoid spaces in the names.

You don't *have* to change page names—sometimes the default name works just fine (such as "Photos" or "Welcome"). This page name also appears in the browser's title bar when the page is viewed.

Rename the site

To rename the site, double-click the word "Site" in the Site Organizer pane. This site name becomes part of the web address, so it's best to use a name that's short with no spaces (such as SweetSwan). Spaces in web addresses are converted into "%20," making an ugly and confusing address (Sweet%20Swan).

Rearrange the pages

The order of the pages in the Site Organizer is the order in which they will appear in the navigation bar across the top of the web page (shown below). **To change the order,** simply drag a page (or a set, such as "Blog" or "Podcast") to another position in the Site Organizer list. The exception is the Welcome page—iWeb insists that it stay as the first page in the navigation, so no matter where you position it in the Site Organizer, it will appear in first place on the web.

This is the navigation bar with links to the other pages in the iWeb site.

Add a link to text or graphics

You can make any photo or graphic element into a link, plus you can make any text into a link. You can create a link to an external page anywhere on the web, to any other page in any of your iWeb sites, to a file on your computer so someone else can download it, or to an email address. Details for each one are in the following directions.

To add a link to text or graphics:

1 If the Inspector isn't showing, click the "Inspector" icon in the bottom-right of the iWeb window to make it appear.

2 In the Inspector, single-click on the "Link Inspector" icon, as shown circled on the opposite page.

3 Select the text that you want to be a link (drag over it) or the graphic image (single-click on it).

4 In the Link Inspector, check the box to "Enable as a hyperlink."

5 From the "Link to" pop-up menu, choose the type of link you want:

And External Page: This link goes to a page anywhere on the web. Just type the address, or copy and paste from a browser.

A File: You can create a link to a file, such as a photograph or a text file; when a visitor clicks the link, the file is automatically downloaded. Make sure the file name is short and sweet because its entire name will appear on the web page and you won't be able to change it.

An Email Message: When a visitor clicks this link, it opens their email application and creates a new message addressed to you with the subject of your choice. Enter the email address and the subject line that you want to appear.

Internal page, called **"One of My Pages":** This is a link to any other page in any of your sites in iWeb.

Create a photo slideshow

Okay, this is so way cool. You won't see the slideshow in iWeb, but after you publish it, you can check it out. People will be so impressed with you. The photos will also automatically appear on an iWeb page called "Photos."

1 First, go to iPhoto and create a new album (Command N). Drag the photos into it that you want to post on your blog site as a slideshow.

   The photos will appear in iWeb in the order they appear in this album, and the titles you give them will also appear (although you can rearrange and rename them in iWeb). The one thing you will not be able to change is this: The first photo in the collection is the one that will appear on the iWeb page that links to the photo page.

2 In iWeb, open the Media Browser, if it isn't already (click the "Media" icon in the bottom-right of the iWeb window).

3 Click the "Photos" tab in the Media Browser.

4 Find the album you just created. Drag the album to the iWeb page and drop it on a photo placeholder, or drop it anywhere on the page (remember, you can add your own graphic border, resize it, etc.).

5 iWeb instantly asks you to choose a new "Photos" page. Click "Choose." On the iWeb page, you see the first photo in the album.

6 iWeb added the new "Photos" page to your site; you can see it in the Site Organizer. Single-click the name of your new page to see your photos all arranged for you! You also see a "Slideshow icon" that you can't click until you publish the site and view it on the web.

   To rearrange the photos on this page, drag them around to new positions.

   To rename the images, single-click on a name and retype.

   To remove a photo, single-click to select it, then hit Delete.

   To add more photos to this same slideshow, drag individual photos or an entire album to the Photos page and drop it.

7 Save your page. When you are ready to publish and check out your slideshow, see Chapter 8.

   (Just click the "Publish" button at the bottom-left of the iWeb window to publish the site to your .Mac account. For details, see Chapter 8.)

Make your site private

You can add a password to your site so only people who know the user name and password can view it. If you have more than one site, you can choose to password-protect individual sites. **To add a password:**

1 If you have more than one iWeb site, click on any *page* in the particular *site* that you want to protect. The password will protect the entire site, no matter which page you choose.

2 Open the Inspector, if it isn't already (click the Inspector button in the bottom-right of the iWeb window).

3 Click the "Site" icon in the Inspector toolbar, as shown to the left. Click the "Password" tab.

4 Check the box to "Make my published site private."

5 Make up a user name and password that visitors will have to enter.

6 Save the site, and when you're ready, publish it as explained in Chapter 8.

   (Just click the "Publish" button at the bottom-left of the iWeb window to publish the site to your .Mac account. For details, see Chapter 8.)

Visitors to your site won't see anything until they enter the user name and password that you assigned.

Use the Inspector palettes

The Inspector palettes provide specifications for seven different categories: Site, Page, Blog & Podcast, Text, Graphic, Metrics, and Link.

First select the item to which you want to apply specifications, then choose the appropriate palette.

Click this button to display the Inspector.

To see the name of each icon in the Inspector toolbar, hover your mouse over the icon (don't click) until the **tool tip** appears, as shown below.

Site Inspector/Site pane

Change the site name.

If you have set up a .Mac Group page, you can publish your iWeb site to the Group page.

This palette also shows how much iDisk storage is available on your .Mac account. Click the "Buy More…" button to add more disk storage space to your account.

Site Inspector/Password pane

To make your site private, click the "Password" tab and set a user name and password. See page 27 for details.

Page Inspector

Change the selected page name and apply other settings that affect page appearance.

To prevent a page from being included in the navigation bar, uncheck "Include page in navigation menu."

If you don't want a certain page to show the navigation bar, uncheck "Display navigation menu."

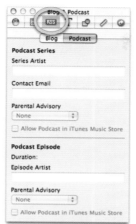

Blog & Podcast Inspector/ Blog pane

Set the number of blog excerpts to show on the main Blog page.

Set the excerpt length (how much of the blog shows on the main Blog page).

If you want to allow others to add comments or attachments, checkmark "Allow comments" or "Allow attachments."

To hide or show a search field on a page, uncheck or check "Display search field."

Blog & Podcast Inspector/ Podcast pane

Enter information about the podcast series and the podcast episode.

The "Series Artist" and "Parental Advisory" are made available to listeners. The "Contact Email" is available only to the publisher of your podcast, in case you need to be contacted.

Check "Allow podcast in iTunes Music Store" to enable submission of your podcast to the iTunes Music Store.

Metrics Inspector

Resize, reposition, rotate, or flip a selected image using controls and numbers instead of dragging with the pointer.

Click "Constrain proportions" if you want to maintain the correct proportions of the image when you resize it. With this checked, you can change the numeric value of either the width or the height and the other measurement will change to match the new proportion.

If you've resized an image and you want it back to its original size, click the "Original Size" button.

Link Inspector

Apply a hyperlink to a selected object or text.

To turn off all links on the iWeb page so you can edit them more easily, check "Make all hyperlinks inactive."

See pages 24–25 for details.

Graphic Inspector

Change the appearance of selected graphics.

Fill a selected object with color, an image, or a pattern.

Apply a stroke (border) and change its color and thickness.

Set a drop shadow on an object and adjust it.

"Reflection" puts a reflection of the selected object on the page.

"Opacity" makes a selected object transparent.

Text Inspector/Text pane

Set text and paragraph attributes for selected text, including color and alignment; the color behind the text ("Background Fill"); the spacing between characters, lines, and paragraphs; and the amount of space to allow between the text and the border of the box it's in (the "Inset Margin").

Text Inspector/Wrap pane

Make text wrap around an object, such as a photo. The object must be inline (pasted into the text) to apply text wrap to it.

Check "Object causes wrap," then choose to align the text to the right or left of the object.

Set the amount of "Extra Space" you want between the object and the text.

Text Inspector/List pane

When you have a list of items on a page, you can tell iWeb to automatically apply bullets to each item, plus you have many controls for the look and position of the bullets.

Ready to Publish?

Once you've played around with creating a few web pages, you're ready to publish your iWeb site and begin your blogging empire.

A typical, ready-to-publish site is shown below. Your site will look different, of course, depending on the template you chose and the content you created.

If you want to wait until you've got a few blog pages ready before you publish your site, go to the next chapter and start blogging!

Or click the "Publish" button at the bottom-left of the iWeb window to publish the existing site to your .Mac account, and add the blogging pages later. See Chapter 8 for details about publishing.

If you see a black dot in the middle of the red button, it means you have not saved the pages.

The red icons indicate pages whose changes have not been published.

Blue page icons indicate pages that are published and up-to-date on the web.

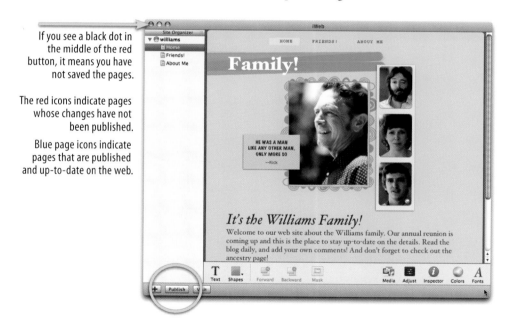

Delete a Site

Perhaps you've been playing around with a practice site and you want to delete it. iWeb won't let you delete the only site in the window, but here's what you can do.

1 If you have only one site, create a new one: From the File menu, choose "New Site." If you already have more than one site, skip to Step 3.

2 Choose a Welcome page for your new site.

3 In the Site Organizer pane, select the name of the site you want to delete. You must select the site itself, not a page in the site! The site is the name with the crystal ball next to it.

4 From the Edit menu, choose "Delete Site."

If the Edit menu doesn't have the option to "Delete Site," but only has the option to "Delete Page," that means the item you selected in the Site Organizer is not the site itself. Try again.

Delete Everything in iWeb

You might want to get rid of everything in iWeb altogether and start from scratch. To do this, you need to delete the file called "Domain.sites."

1 Go to the Finder and open a Finder window.

2 View the window by Columns (click in the little "Column View" icon in the toolbar).

3 In the Sidebar, single-click on your home icon. In the next column, **single-click** on "Library," then "Application Support," then "iWeb," then "Domain.sites." This is the file that holds everything you've ever created in iWeb. Delete this file and iWeb will act like it's never been opened before.

Follow this path to find the Domain file.

Blog On!
Blog Louder!

If you're comfortable with iWeb, let's start blogging! You'll be amazed at how easy it is. This chapter assumes you know how to edit text and graphics, as explained in detail in Chapter 2.

These are the steps you'll go through to set up your blog:

1 Create a "Blog" set of pages in your new site.

2 Edit the text and graphics on the "Entries" page.

3 Click the button to publish it.

Create a Blog!

Okay, there is lots more to tell you about designing the pages in iWeb, but we know your point in reading this book is to set up a blog (and/or a podcast). So let's do it. We assume you now have a Welcome page and that you feel fairly comfortable with editing the text and graphics.

To add a blog page:

1 In iWeb, click the **+** button at the bottom-left of the screen.

2 In the sheet that drops down, shown below, your template master is probably already highlighted on the left (if not, find it and single-click on it).

On the right side of the pane, double-click on the "Blog" page, shown circled below.

3 Now edit your blog as you learned in Chapter 2 (see the opposite page)!

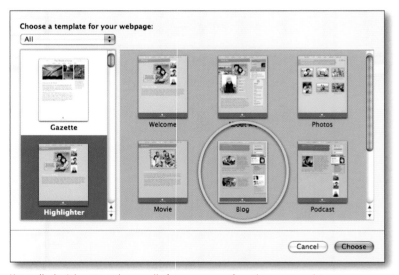

You really don't have to make sure all of your pages are from the same template—feel free to mix and match.

Edit your Blog

The "Entries" page shows up waiting for you to replace the existing text with your own words. In the example below, the title of the blog is even highlighted for you. Replace, edit, and customize the text and graphics just as you learned in the previous chapter.

The "Blog" page you added is actually a collection of three pages, as you can see in the Site Organizer below: Blog, Entries, and Archive. Each of these pages has a very important and separate purpose, explained on the following pages.

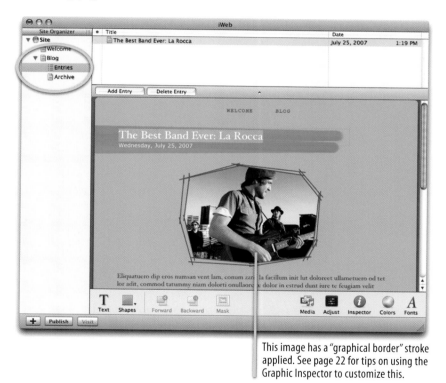

This image has a "graphical border" stroke applied. See page 22 for tips on using the Graphic Inspector to customize this.

The "Blog" Set of Pages

When you add a Blog, iWeb actually adds a *set* of three pages, as you can see in the Site Organizer. Each of these pages has a very important function. Click the link in the Site Organizer to show the page.

The "Blog" page

This is the page your visitors will see on your site once it's posted to the web. You can edit everything on this page *except* the blog itself, the piece you see circled in the graphic below. You can't edit this because iWeb automatically generates this from your blog entry, as shown on the next page. You can resize this text block or move it, *but don't delete it.*

To publish your site so you can check it out along the way, just click the "Publish" button at the bottom-left of the iWeb window and it will publish to your .Mac account. For details, see Chapter 8.

The "Entries" page

This is where you will update your blog. Whenever you feel so inclined, come to the *Entries* page, add a new entry, edit the text and graphics, and publish.

> **Make a new entry:** Click the button "Add Entry," then replace the existing text and graphics.

> **Delete an entry:** Select an entry name in the top list of entries, then click the "Delete Entry" button.

> **Change the date:** You can pre- or post-date your entries by double-clicking on the date in the upper-right column. Change the date, then click anywhere on the iWeb page.

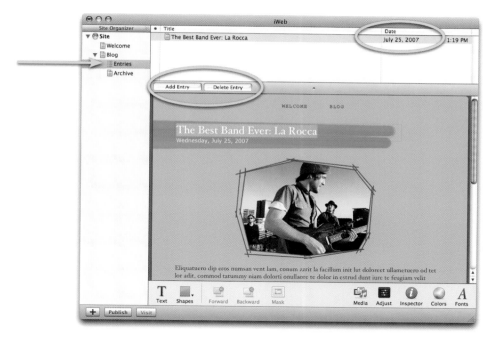

The "Archive" page

iWeb updates this page whenever you add a new blog entry. *You can't do anything to this page* except change the title and rearrange items. iWeb automatically generates this page and the text, based on your blogs.

When visitors to your blog click the "Go to Archive" button on your blog page, it takes them to this *Archive* page where iWeb has created linked excerpts of each blog. (You control how much of the excerpt is visible on the Archives page using the Blog Inspector; see page 29.)

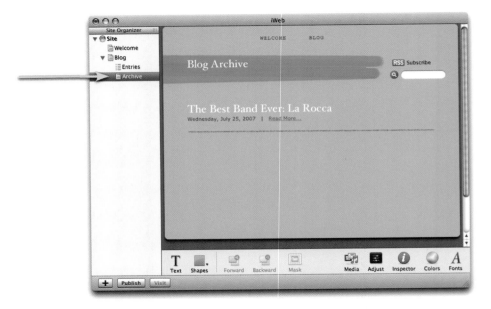

Allow comments on your blog

Many bloggers like to allow visitors to add their own comments. iWeb allows you to add this feature to your blogs, and also gives you the ability to delete visitor comments, if necessary. You can also allow visitors to post attachments, such as photos or files, for other people to access on your blog.

To allow comments and attached files on your blog page:

1   In iWeb, go to the Site Organizer and click on the main blog page titled "Blog."

2   If the Inspector isn't showing, click the "Inspector" icon in the bottom-right of the iWeb window to make it appear.

3   In the Inspector, single-click on the "Blog & Podcast" icon, as shown below, then make sure the "Blog" tab is selected.

4   Check the box to "Allow comments."

If you want to allow visitors to upload attachments, check that box as well.

5   Save and publish your site (click the "Publish" button at the bottom-left of the iWeb window; see Chapter 8 for details).

—continued

Visitors will now see a link to "ADD A COMMENT," as shown below.

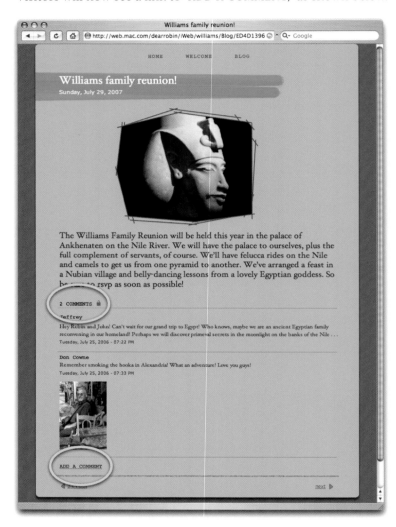

Add a comment

When visitors go to your page and click the link to add a comment, they will get a window like the one shown on the opposite page. They'll type their comment and sign a name in the "Comment as" field. If they add a URL (web address), their name becomes a link that goes to that web address. If they add an email address, their name becomes an email link.

Every commenter must enter the characters shown in the blue image to prevent automated spam from showing up on your blog.

If you have allowed attachments, the commenter can click the blue link to "Add Attachment." The "Choose File" button appears, as shown below-right. The commenter clicks the button, finds the file they want to upload, and off it goes. You can see on the opposite page an example of a photo that someone uploaded (attached) to the blog page.

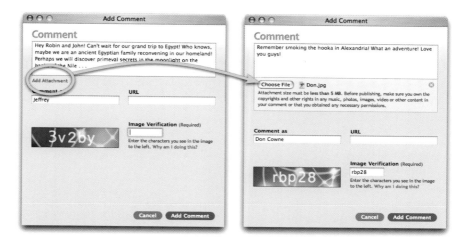

You've got comments!

When someone posts a comment, iWeb tells you in two ways—*if* iWeb is open on your Mac. The icon in the Dock displays a number, like the Mail application, telling you how many new comments have been posted. And the Site Organizer in iWeb displays a blue dot next to the Blog page that has new comments.

Delete a comment

On the opposite page, you can see a lock icon next to the number of comments. Click that lock icon, enter your .Mac account name and password, and you can choose to delete any comment.

All Done?

Once you've written your blog and designed the site pages, you're ready to publish your iWeb site and begin your blogging empire. A typical, ready-to-publish site is shown below. Your site will look different, of course, depending on the template you chose and the content you created.

You can click the "Publish" button at the bottom-left of the iWeb window to publish the site to your .Mac account, or see Chapter 8 if you want more details first.

The selected blog entry is shown in the window below.

The page icons' red color indicates that the current changes have not yet been published.

Blue pages do not have any *unpublished* changes.

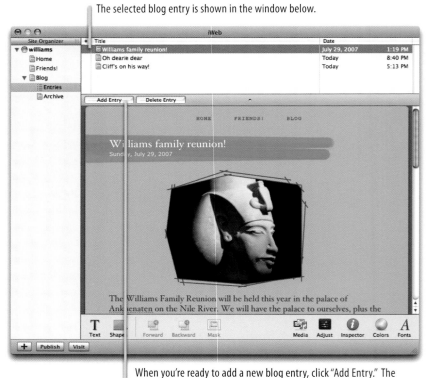

When you're ready to add a new blog entry, click "Add Entry." The new blog is automatically added to the list on the main "Blog" page.

To Update your Blog

Add a new entry, then click the Publish button!

Plan your Podcast

Preliminary planning and preparation can save lots of time in the creation of a podcast project. Most importantly, the quality of podcast content usually improves with a little well-thought-out planning.

While improvisation and ad-libbing may have its own charm, you'll benefit from following a few guidelines and procedures to help enable a smooth and efficient production of your podcast episodes.

Plan your Episodes

If you like, you can create random podcasts about a wide variety of subjects, publishing them with unpredictable and undependable schedules. But if you want to build a successful podcast with a following and subscribers, try to develop a consistent theme for the episodes you create, and publish each new episode on a timely basis, following a consistent schedule. If you're planning a personal podcast about family news, this may not seem too important. However, even family members will be more likely to keep up with your podcast if they know it's on a schedule.

A podcast doesn't have to be forever. You can decide how many episodes you want to include in a podcast series, then end it. You can always extend the series "due to popular demand." Or change to another subject. The point is that it's much less intimidating to commit to a short-term podcast schedule—once a month for six months, for instance—than it is to a commitment with an eternal schedule. If you just want to have fun and don't care about building a loyal audience, publish an episode whenever you like.

Some podcasters publish every day, some weekly or monthly. You might even decide you want to publish an annual podcast for your family that replaces the goofy poem you write every year that updates the relatives on all your achievements of the past year. If they liked the written version, imagine how they'll react to the podcasting version with background music and visuals. You'll be famous—or at least talked-about.

Decide on a podcasting style

When you're ready to record your podcast, you might want to decide in advance what style of presentation to use.

One approach is to have a very tight script that you follow closely. Another is to have a rough outline of topics you want to talk about, while avoiding a formal, rehearsed presentation.

You can also "wing it" and just ad-lib your way through the recording with random thoughts and musings, then get rid of the mistakes and awkward parts in the editing phase of production. If you're good at ad-libbing and improvisational speaking, this style can be fun and entertaining.

For most of us, it's best to have at least a rough outline to follow. If you're going to have a guest on your podcast, be sure to have plenty of prepared questions, and be familiar with the subject they plan to discuss. An outline of your episode helps to organize your presentation and ensure that you have time to cover everything you hope to discuss during the recording session.

Plan a reasonable podcast duration

Most podcasts are twenty to thirty minutes long, at the most. Longer durations may cause listeners to lose interest and get bored. Of course, if you run a few minutes over, no one's going to get in trouble. It's the Internet, after all—it's not as if your podcast is going to delay a CNN breaking news report.

A longer podcast also means a larger audio file that takes up more storage space on your server and uses more bandwidth to play on the Internet. If you have a large audience, bandwidth usage can add up, sometimes resulting in extra charges from your Internet Service Provider for exceeding the allotted amount covered by your contract. This likely won't be an issue until your podcast becomes wildly successful. If your podcast does become that successful, you can sell advertising space on your web page to offset the bandwidth fees.

Organize your Assets

It's easy to add photos, graphics, songs, and movies to your blogs and podcasts.

Even though you can drag various media from any location on your computer into an iWeb template or into GarageBand's "Podcast Track," it will be much easier to find and place these assets if you first organize them before you start your project. Both iWeb and GarageBand include a Media Browser that provides instant access to iPhoto, iTunes, and your Movies folder. A little time spent on organizing your assets so they appear in the Media Browser will make them easier to access.

iWeb and its floating Media Browser.

GarageBand and its built-in Media Browser.

Organize your photos and graphics

In iPhoto, create one or more new albums for blog or podcast images. Drag the photos you plan to use into the new albums. If you've prepared other types of graphics, you can drag those into the new iPhoto album as well.

Organize your songs

If you plan to add links to songs on an iWeb page or place a music file in GarageBand, drag those music files into a new iTunes playlist that's named for your blog or podcast project.

Organize your movies

The Media Browsers in iWeb and GarageBand look for movie files in the Movies folder of your Home folder, as well as in iTunes. If you have movies stored in other folders, just click the "Movies" tab at the top of the Media Browser and drag other movies folders from your Desktop into the "Movies" pane (shown below).

Note: Drag movie clips to the GarageBand window only if you're making a video podcast rather than a standard podcast. You can put *either* still images or movie files in GarageBand's top track, but not *both*.

Drag a movie file from the Media Browser to the top track. If the top track was a "Podcast Track," it is converted to a "Video Track."

Drag a folder of movies from anywhere on your computer into the Movies pane of the Media Browser.

—continued

Now you're organized!

Instead of searching for assets that are scattered all over your hard disk and other external disks, everything you need shows up in the Media Browser.

Movie clips stored in a folder that was dragged to the top pane of the Media Browser are displayed in the bottom pane. Movies or movie clips can be dragged from the bottom pane to an iWeb page.

The same Media Browser shows the contents of iTunes when you select the "Audio" tab. Songs or playlists can be dragged to an iWeb page. Commercial songs do not actually play on the iWeb page—they are linked to the iTunes Music Store.

You're Ready!

Trust us, organizing things before you start makes the process much less frustrating. You'll progress faster and feel more confident.

So onward! Amaze the podcasting world!

Record your Podcast

Production of your podcast starts with the processs of recording your voice in GarageBand. We assume you read the minimum requirements on page 3 and you've installed the latest version of Apple's iLife software (which includes GarageBand and iWeb).

Here are the steps you'll take to record the primary content of your podcast—your voice commentary:

1 Choose a microphone.

2 Create a "New Podcast Episode" in GarageBand.

3 Set GarageBand's audio preferences, plus the audio input level in your System Preferences.

4 Record your commentary.

These steps are explained in detail on the following pages. When you complete these first steps, you're ready to edit and mix your podcast (explained in Chapter 6).

Overview of GarageBand's Features

GarageBand combines three audio-editing tools into one: a **recorder,** an **editor,** and a **mixer:**

When a microphone is connected, you can **record** your voice (or any kind of sound) in GarageBand and it gets placed in a soundtrack timeline. You can **edit** the soundtrack, silence certain sections of the audio, delete pieces, add sections, and rearrange it. Then **mix** it—add sound effects and sound filters, and control the volume of different audio elements (a jingle intro or mood music playing under a voice, for instance).

You can create individual soundtracks for the various audio elements you may want to use, such as theme music, jingles, or sound effects. And, as you'll see, GarageBand even includes a special timeline track for graphics. This lets you place photos or graphics in your podcast that appear at the exact point in the podcast that you specify. It's a drag-and-drop operation, so it's easy and fun.

Suggestion: We suggest you follow the steps in these chapters to first create a **practice podcast.** If it's a practice piece, you will concentrate on learning to use the tools instead of trying to make it perfect!

You Need a Microphone

You can use your computer's built-in microphone, if it has one (all newer model Macs have them). Built-in mics aren't meant to deliver professional sound quality, but they're good enough for learning how to podcast.

How do you know if your Mac has a built-in microphone? It's not easy to tell by looking at it. If your Mac has a built-in iSight camera, it includes a microphone. If you have a laptop, you might see a tiny little hole somewhere on the frame around the keyboard or the monitor—that's probably the microphone.

You can always **check the Sound preferences** to see if you've got an internal microphone:

1 Go to the Apple menu, choose "System Preferences…," then click the "Sound" icon.

2 Click the "Input" tab.

3 In the "Input" pane (shown below), if you see "Internal microphone . . . Built-in," you've got a mic.

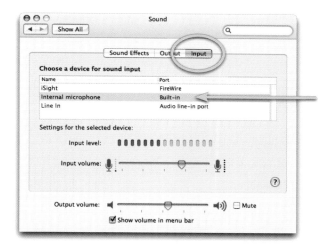

If you don't see an option for a built-in microphone, you can use an external iSight camera, or you can buy an inexpensive mic for about $30 that plugs into one of your USB ports.

If you enjoy podcasting and want to invest in better audio quality, consider purchasing a really nice external microphone. For information about these and other options, please see Chapter 10.

Because you're probably anxious to get started, we're going to move forward assuming you'll be using your Mac's built-in microphone.

Create a New Podcast Episode

In podcasting, a single podcast is called an **episode;** a collection of episodes is a **series.** We're going to create an episode.

1 Open GarageBand. (If GarageBand is already open, go to the File menu and choose "New.")

   In the window that opens (below-left), click the "New Podcast Episode" icon.

2 In the "New Project from Template" window (bottom-right), name the episode and choose where you want to save it.

   The default location for saving an episode is the GarageBand folder, which is inside the Music folder that's in your Home folder (shown below-right). You can choose to save the GarageBand file to any location you want, but if you don't have an excellent reason for saving it somewhere else, let GarageBand put it in its folder.

3 Click the "Create" button.

The GarageBand podcast window opens, as shown on the opposite page. GarageBand automatically creates five different **tracks** to hold the audio files in your podcast. You don't have to use them all, and you can create additional tracks if you need them.

The top **track** ("Podcast Track") actually holds graphics that will display with your podcast (see Chapter 6). Notice that when you single-click on this track, it's purple.

The next two tracks are for recording voices. When you single-click on one of these to select it, it's blue.

The bottom two tracks are for jingles and sound effects. When you click on the Jingles track, it's blue; the Radio Sounds track is green. We'll explain these color codes in a minute.

You probably see the "Track Editor" on the bottom half of your GarageBand window, as shown below. If you don't, click the Track Editor button (shown circled). You don't have to have this visible to record, though.

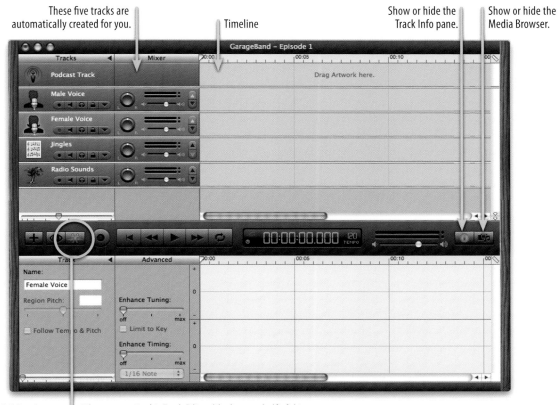

These five tracks are automatically created for you.

Timeline

Show or hide the Track Info pane.

Show or hide the Media Browser.

Track Editor button.

What you see in this Track Editor (the bottom half of this window) depends on which track you have chosen above.

Set GarageBand Preferences

Before you go any further, you need to customize a few of the settings in GarageBand preferences and in the System Preferences.

GarageBand preferences

We'll ignore some of the settings in GarageBand preferences that are for creating or composing music. The following settings directly affect your podcast recording.

To open the GarageBand preferences, go to GarageBand's application menu and choose "Preferences…."

You'll see the pane shown below. Read the following pages and set your preferences.

General preferences

There are times when you'll need to send a project to iTunes. To enable GarageBand to **export files to iTunes,** you must first enter a playlist name, composer name, and album name in the "General" preferences window.

The information you enter will appear in your iTunes window (under the playlist name you enter), making it easy to find your GarageBand projects and songs. When you need to import a recording you made into iMovie, iWeb, or another GarageBand project, this playlist will be accessible in those other applications through each one's "Media Browser."

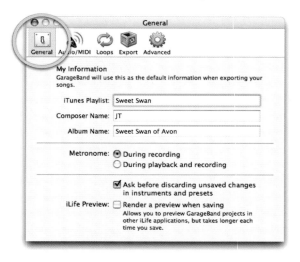

Audio/MIDI preferences

Before you start recording, you need to check some settings in GarageBand's "Audio" preferences.

1 If your preferences are not still open, go to the GarageBand menu and choose "Preferences…."

2 Click the "Audio/MIDI" icon.

MIDI (Musical Instrument Digital Interface) is a **Software Instrument** protocol that describes musical sounds as digital information that a computer can interpret and play.

3 Use the **Audio Output** pop-up menu to choose the speakers you want to use:

> "Built-in Audio" (or "Built-in Output) refers to your computer's **built-in speakers.**

> If you have **external speakers** connected, their name appears as an option in the menu.

4 Most importantly, you must tell GarageBand which **microphone** you are going to use for recording: From the **Audio Input** pop-up menu, choose the microphone you want to use. If you have an external mic connected, you'll see its name here. If you have a mic connected to an audio interface (see Chapter 10), it also appears in this pop-up menu.

—continued

If you change the "Audio Input" setting to another microphone, the sheet shown below appears. Click "Yes."

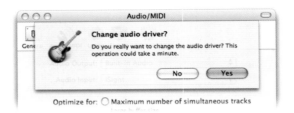

5 The **Optimize for** settings in this Audio/MIDI pane are to reduce "latency." Latency is a small delay that may be heard when playing or recording your podcast in GarageBand (especially on an older, slower computer). It takes a tiny bit of time for a recorded voice or instrument to go from the mic to the computer's input port and be processed. **To reduce latency,** choose "Minimum delay when playing instruments live."

You can close the preferences now.

Sound Settings

Before you record, set the input level for your microphone. This helps determine how loud your voice will be when you record it in GarageBand.

1 Click the System Preferences icon in the Dock (shown to the left), or go to the Apple menu and choose "System Preferences…."

2 Click the "Sound" icon.

3 In the "Sound" window, click the "Input" tab.

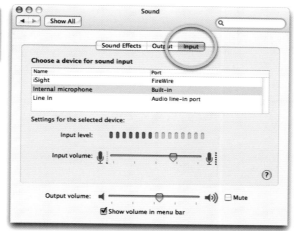

4 Select the microphone that you want to use for sound input.

5 Move the "Input level" slider to the right to raise the mic's volume; move it left to lower its volume. Speak into the mic in a normal voice to check the input level. When you speak, the blue lights indicate the strength of the input level. Depending on the mic you use, you may have to move the slider quite far to the right to avoid a weak signal (volume too low). If the level is set too high, the audio may be distorted.

6 The "Output volume" slider sets the volume of your speakers. Check the box to "Show volume in menu bar" so you can easily access this control while you're working.

As you work on your podcast, you can return to this Sound preferences window at any time to adjust your microphone's input volume.

Test your Microphone

In GarageBand, test the sound levels by talking toward the microphone. Follow these steps:

First, select a track: Single-click on the track "header," shown below. GarageBand has already applied filters to the "Male Voice" and "Female Voice," tracks that are optimized for those voices.

Speak into the microphone and watch the level indicators (circled below) as you record.

If the tiny lights on the right side of the level indicators turn red, **clipping** (sound distortion) is occuring. **To prevent clipping,** either:

> Lower the input level of the mic (see the previous page).

> Lower the volume of the track that you've selected (adjust the slider circled below).

> Move the mic further away from yourself.

When you select a **voice track,** it turns blue. (Other tracks turn other colors.)

This area is the track header.

If you don't see the Mixer column, click the tiny triangle in the Tracks column label.

Record your Podcast

Now you can start the fun part—recording your podcast. Get your script, outline, or notes if you have any of these. Since this is a recording, you don't have to worry about making mistakes—you can re-record anything you want and edit as much as needed after the basic recording is finished. Remember, it might be less stressful to create a practice podcast first!

1 **Select the track** you want to record on. The track turns blue to show it's selected. The **red dot** on the left side of the controls indicates that recording is enabled for this track (if the dot is not red, single-click on it).

The "Male Voice" and the "Female Voice" tracks are optimized for male or female voices, but you can use either one you want.

Or you can get rid of either one (select it, then hit Command Delete, or go the the Track menu and choose "Delete Track").

—continued

2 When you record, the audio will be placed in the timeline beginning wherever the **Playhead** is positioned. **To make sure the Playhead is at the beginning of the track,** click the "Go to the Beginning" button. Or drag the Playhead itself all the way to the left.

3 **To start recording:** Click the Record button and speak into the microphone. As you speak, your recorded voice appears as a purple *region* in the timeline and contains a graphic audio waveform. (If the waveform is flat, your microphone isn't turned on, or perhaps you didn't set the input Sound preferences as explained on pages 55–56.)

4 **To stop recording:** Click the blue triangle to stop the recording and to stop the Playhead from moving on. (You can also click the red Record button to stop recording, but the Playhead will keep moving.)

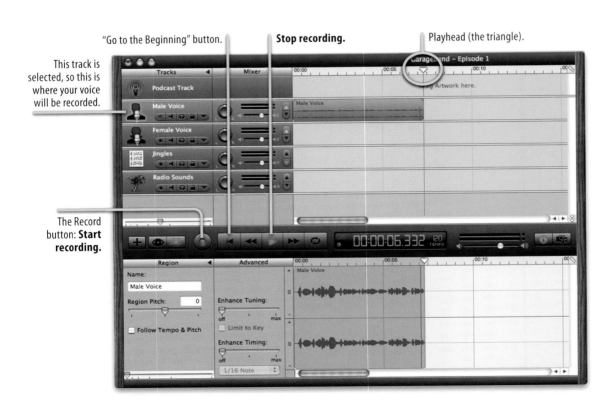

"Go to the Beginning" button.

Stop recording.

Playhead (the triangle).

This track is selected, so this is where your voice will be recorded.

The Record button: **Start recording.**

Listen to your Recording

Of course, you'll want to listen to what you recorded before you start the editing process. **To listen to what you recorded,** choose one of these methods:

> First, make sure the Playhead is stopped.
>
> Then, send the Playhead back to the beginning of the timeline: Click the "Go to the beginning" button.
>
> To listen to your recording, click the Playback button, the big triangle. When you've heard all you want, click the Playback button again to stop the Playhead.

> **Or** click the "Go to the beginning" button to send the Playhead to the beginning, then hit the Spacebar to start and stop playback.

> **Or** hit any one of these three keys to send the Playhead back to the beginning: Z, Home, or Return.
>
> Now hit the Spacebar to start the playback. When you hit one of the three keys above, the playback will start over again and keep repeating every time you hit the key. When you're sick and tired of listening to it, hit the Spacebar again to stop the playback.

If you like using keyboard shortcuts, here's where you'll find a lengthy list of them: In GarageBand, go to the Help menu and choose "Keyboard Shortcuts."

Audio Clips are Called Regions

As you're recording, you can stop and start as often as you like; each time you start and stop you create an individual **region,** as shown below. Later, while editing, you can easily rearrange, copy, or delete these regions.

In the timeline, you see two separate regions. It's easy to record these short audio clips, then drag them around in the timeline.

You can stop recording at any time, then record a new region at the point where you made a mistake. Just because you record something doesn't mean you have to use it!

As you'll learn in the next chapter, editing mistakes, throwing away unwanted audio, and putting together multiple sound clips so they sound like one continuous podcast is really easy.

After you've recorded the basic content of your podcast, you can add audio filters to improve the sound quality. Putting music or sound effects on other tracks makes it easy to overlap audio clips and create a podcast that sounds professional.

For now, create a short recording with a few regions in it that you can work with in the next chapter to practice editing.

More Than One Voice?

So far we've shown how to record one voice onto one audio track. Many podcasts consist of just that. You might, however, want to include other voices, perhaps inserting an interview or a casual conversation. The easiest way to record two or more people is to gather everyone closely around a single microphone and record all their voices on the same track.

But there are several other ways to record multiple voices, with each voice on its own audio track. This technique provides more editing flexibility—you can do things like lower the volume of a selected voice or remove certain comments on one track without affecting the sound on other tracks. See Chapter 10 to learn how to use multiple microphones to record simultaneously on multiple tracks.

Edit & Mix your Podcast

After you record all of the sound clips you need for your podcast, you'll **edit** the clips to create a more professional presentation. You can delete unwanted comments or noises, such as your dog begging for a biscuit in the middle of a recording or a phone ringing in the background. You can remove long pauses that occurred while recording when you lost your train of thought, or replace sections of audio that contain mistakes.

Mixing is also part of the editing process, when you add filters, jingles, or sound effects, and (in the case of podcasting with GarageBand), add graphics and chapter markers that make your podcast more interesting, useful, entertaining, and professional.

To review: A sound clip in a track is called a **region.** There can be many regions in a single track. When you record audio for your podcast, you can create many short sound clips or a couple of long ones.

Some projects need more editing and mixing than others—especially if you use lots of jingles or sound effects. On the other hand, you could possibly get by with no editing or mixing at all. But, as you'll see, at least minimal editing and mixing usually improves your podcast.

The GarageBand Controls

Before you start editing, take a moment to become familiar with the various controls in GarageBand. Below, you see the Control Bar and its features.

Go to beginning.

Show Loop Browser (see pages 65 and 79).

Show Track Editor (see page 65).

Start/Stop playback.

Cycle region (see page 66).

Time display.

Show Track Info (see page 67).

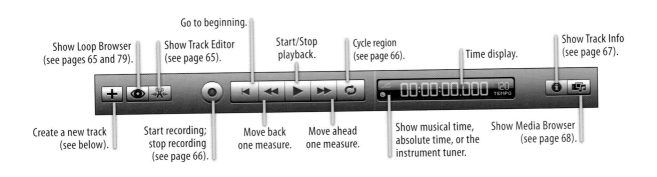

Create a new track (see below).

Start recording; stop recording (see page 66).

Move back one measure.

Move ahead one measure.

Show musical time, absolute time, or the instrument tuner.

Show Media Browser (see page 68).

Main controls

Show or hide certain panes, create new tracks when necessary, and preview your podcast.

Create a new track

Since GarageBand automatically creates several "Real Instrument" tracks when you open a new podcast project, you don't need to create any new tracks for a basic podcast. But when you're ready, click this button to create a new audio track. You'll be asked to choose the type of track you want to create:

Software Instrument track: For musical notes created using an onscreen keyboard, a MIDI keyboard, or some other MIDI instrument.

Real Instrument track: Audio recordings of voices or instruments captured by a microphone, as well as other audio capture devices.

Show the Loop Browser

This button shows (or hides) the Loop Browser (as shown on page 79), where you'll find a collection of music and sounds that you can drag to a track. Use the three buttons in the bottom-left corner of the Loop Browser to view the items in different ways—as *text columns, musical buttons,* or *podcast sounds.* Click the *podcast sounds* button to access audio loops provided for podcasting.

Click here to show the podcast sounds in the Loop Browser.

 Show the Track Editor

Click this button to show or hide the **Track Editor** (shown below). What you see in the Track Editor depends on which track is *selected.* Below is a sample of a voice track. This close-up view makes it easier to edit small sections of audio.

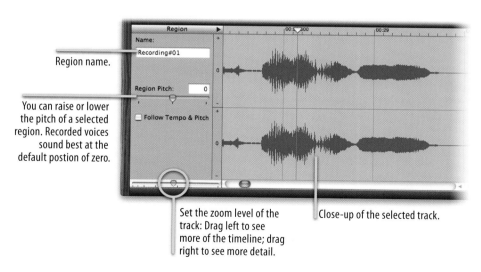

Region name.

You can raise or lower the pitch of a selected region. Recorded voices sound best at the default postion of zero.

Set the zoom level of the track: Drag left to see more of the timeline; drag right to see more detail.

Close-up of the selected track.

Start/Stop recording

To record, click the red button. **To stop recording,** click the button again.

Or hit the R key to start or stop recording (although when you hit the R key to stop recording, the Playhead continues moving; to stop recording *and* stop the Playhead from moving on, hit the Spacebar).

Playback buttons

These buttons control the playback of your project.

The first button on the left moves the Playhead to the beginning of the timeline.

The double-arrow buttons move the Playhead back or ahead one *measure.* Each tic mark at the top of the timeline is a measure. The actual duration of a measure changes according to the current zoom level of the track (shown on the previous page).

The big triangle button starts and stops playback.

Cycle region button

The **cycle region button** (the loop icon in the Playback buttons) lets you designate a segment of the timeline to loop (repeat) over and over. This is useful when you want to hear the same section of audio repeated while you experiment with different effects or settings.

To choose the segment you want to loop:

1 Click the "cycle region" button.

2 An orange bar appears at the top of the timeline. Drag the edges of the orange bar to include the area of the timeline you want to loop.

3 Start the playback (you can hit the Spacebar) and it will repeat over and over until you stop the playback (hit the Spacebar again).

Show Track Info

Click this button to show or hide the the Track Info pane on the right side of the GarageBand window. The Track Info pane contains settings for many different sound filters and effects. See pages 84–89 for more information.

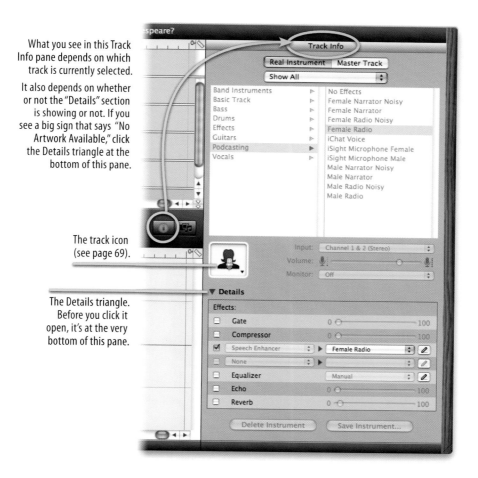

What you see in this Track Info pane depends on which track is currently selected.

It also depends on whether or not the "Details" section is showing or not. If you see a big sign that says "No Artwork Available," click the Details triangle at the bottom of this pane.

The track icon (see page 69).

The Details triangle. Before you click it open, it's at the very bottom of this pane.

 Show Media Browser

Click this button to show or hide the Media Browser on the right side of the GarageBand window. From the Media Browser you can drag audio, photos, or movies into your podcast project.

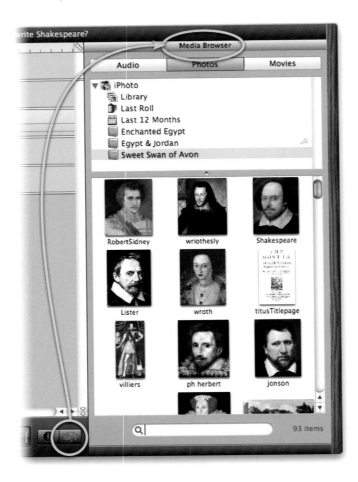

Track controls

Each track has controls that affect only that track. This area of controls is called the **header.**

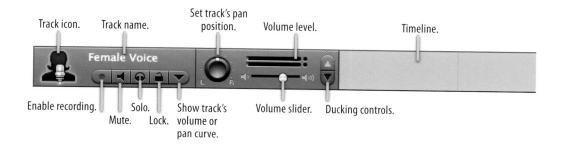

Track icon.   Track name.   Set track's pan position.   Volume level.   Timeline.

Enable recording.   Mute.   Solo.   Lock.   Show track's volume or pan curve.   Volume slider.   Ducking controls.

Track icon: To change this icon, click the icon well in the Track Info pane (above the "Details" triangle, shown on page 67) and choose an icon from the palette.

Track name: To rename a track, select that track. Double-click on the current name to select it, then type a new one.

However, if you choose a different instrument for a selected track (see pages 84–85), the name changes to the new instrument. So it's kind of a waste of time to change its name until the very end of your project.

Enable recording: To record on a track, this button must be red. If it's not red, click once on it.

Mute: To mute (or unmute) a track.

Solo: To hear only one track and mute all others.

Lock track: To prevent changes to a track, click this. This "renders" the track to your hard drive, freeing up your computer's processing power.

Show volume or pan curve: To show the track's volume or pan curve. See page 78 for details.

—continued

Set track's pan position. Volume level.

Volume slider. Ducking controls.

Mixer tools

If you don't see the mixer tools as shown above (in the right-hand part of the header), click the tiny triangle in the "Tracks" column heading, as shown on page 77.

Set pan position: This dial sets the balance of sound between left and right speakers for the entire track.

Volume level: The top bars display the volume level of recording and playback. If the level is too high, the clipping indicator lights on the right turn red.

Volume slider: This sets a volume for the entire track; slide it left or right.

Ducking control: GarageBand's ducking feature automatically lowers the volume of a backing track when a lead track is playing. See pages 82–83.

Edit your Podcast

There are many ways to edit your podcast. Following are the techniques you'll use most often.

Modify regions

Each individual sound clip in an audio track is called a **region.** Each time you start and stop the recording, you create an individual region. Think of regions as the building blocks of a podcast. They can be modified and rearranged, many times if necessary. Modifications you make to a region can always be undone; this is known as "non-destructive" editing.

Important note: When you press-and-drag a region to move it left or right, you might expect the timeline to behave like your Dock or an application's toolbar, scooting all the other items over to make room. GarageBand doesn't do that!

When you drag a region to move it to the right, for instance, you can drop it anywhere in the timeline, *but the region on which you dropped it doesn't move over—its contents get overwritten (you won't hear the recording).*

So you always need to **move the other regions out of the way** before you paste a region into a new position, before you rearrange regions, etc. Just select all the regions to the right of where you want to insert something, and move them all over to create a space in which to insert.

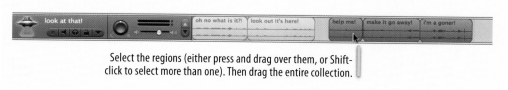

Select the regions (either press and drag over them, or Shift-click to select more than one). Then drag the entire collection.

—continued

Split a long recording into smaller regions

You might have recorded one long audio segment that you want to separate into smaller pieces so you have more flexibility in rearranging the clips, adding pauses, etc. Here's how to separate it:

1 Click on the region in the timeline to select it.

2 Position the Playhead at the point in the timeline where you want to begin the separation.

3 Press Command T (or go to the Edit menu and choose "Split").

4 Continue to move the Playhead to positions, then press Command T to separate at that point.

Rearrange regions

You can rearrange regions in the timeline. First move the other regions to make room for the new position, as explained on the previous page. Then, **to rearrange a region,** press on it and drag it to the empty position in the timeline.

Cut and paste regions

1 Select a region.

2 Press Command X to cut it.

3 Create the space in which to paste this region, as explained on the previous page.

4 Position the Playhead where you want to paste in the region.

5 Press Command V to paste. You might need to readjust the positions of the other regions.

Duplicate regions

Also see page 80 about making jingles loop (repeat).

You may want to duplicate a region; for instance, you might want a sound effect to last longer. **To duplicate a region,** just copy and paste it, as explained above, but press Command **C** to **copy** the selected region (instead of Command **X** to cut it).

Or Option-drag: Hold down the Option key, then press-and-drag the region to duplicate and move it.

Remember, you must first create a space for the region, as explained on the previous page!

Shorten a region's duration

When you shorten a region's duration, you're not condensing it so it *sounds* faster—you are *eliminating* the sound in whatever section you shorten. This is non-destructive, though, meaning that you can easily recover whatever you eliminated.

1 Place the pointer over the bottom half of a region's edge. Whether you choose the right or the left edge, of course, depends on which end of the region you want to eliminate sound from.

When the pointer is in the correction position, it changes to a *resize* pointer (shown below).

Resize pointer.

2 With the resize pointer, drag the edge toward the middle of the selected region to shorten it.

To recover the removed audio, use the resize pointer to drag the region's edge back out to the right.

Delete a region

To delete an entire region, select it, then hit the Delete key. The space in the timeline where that region used to sit will now be a pause, a blank space. If you don't want a pause there, select and move all the regions over to fill the empty space.

Delete just part of a region

To delete just part of a region, you need to first separate that piece. This is essentially a different way to do the same thing you did on page 72, where you split a long region into separate parts.

1 Select the region in the timeline to show it in the Track Editor.

2 If you don't see the Track Editor at the bottom of the window, double-click in the region and the Track Editor will appear (or click the Track Editor button, as shown on page 65).

3 Position the pointer low enough in the Track Editor for the pointer to turn into a crosshair, as shown below.

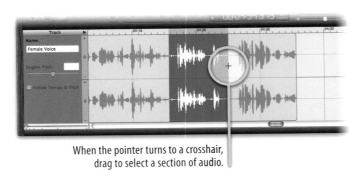

When the pointer turns to a crosshair,
drag to select a section of audio.

4 With that crosshair, select the section of audio you want to delete by dragging across it, as shown below (you'll have to listen to it a few times to figure out where you want to select).

5 Click once on the selection to turn it into a separate region.

6 Now that it's a separate region and it's selected, just hit the Delete key to get rid of it. This creates a blank spot in your track, so if you don't want a pause here, move the other regions over to fill the spot.

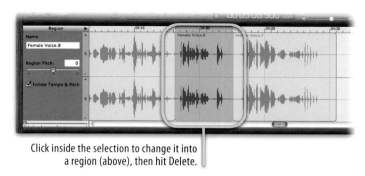

Click inside the selection to change it into
a region (above), then hit Delete.

Remember, this is *non-destructive editing*. Even though you delete a region, the region next to the deleted one still contains what you thought you deleted. **To get the deleted sounds back,** just drag the edge of the region next to the deleted one and it will reappear.

Add a pause between regions

To put a pause between two regions, select all the regions *to the right* of where you want to add the pause. Then drag that *selected* group of regions to the right to add space between it and the previous region.

This blank space indicates a
pause in the playback.

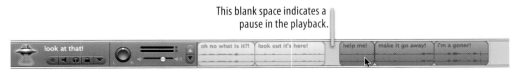

Select all the regions to the right, then
move the entire group to create a pause.

To shorten a pause between regions, drag a region closer to an adjacent region.

To remove a pause between two regions, butt them against each other in the timeline.

Overlapping: If you drag a region and it overlaps another region, the *selected* region (the one you dragged) *replaces* the overlapped section of the other region. **To recover audio that was replaced by the overlapping region,** place the pointer over the bottom half of the region's edge so the pointer changes to a *resize* pointer (as shown on page 73). Use the resize pointer to drag the edge of the region back out to its original duration.

Undo and revert

As in many other Mac applications, you can **undo** a number of actions. Generally, you can keep hitting Command Z to undo actions you've made—*up until the last time you saved the file.*

To get rid of everything you've done since the last time you saved, go to the File menu and choose "Revert to Saved." Anything you did since you last saved the file will be gone. That means you should consciously save when you think you're at a great point and you don't want to lose it.

If you rarely save the file, you are asking for trouble! The mere inaction of not saving can eventually cause you to crash. SOS: Save Often, Sweetie!

Adjust a track's volume and pan settings

Volume, of course, refers to the sound levels. **Pan** refers to the balance of sound between the left and right speakers.

To adjust the volume and pan, you need the **Mixer** column visible, as shown below. If you don't see it, click the tiny triangle on the right edge of the "Tracks" column heading.

Click this triangle to show (or to hide) the Mixer column.

Pan control.　　Volume slider.

To adjust volume and pan settings for the *entire track,* use the volume slider and pan control found in the Mixer column, shown above.

As you edit an audio track, you might realize that what you really need is to lower the volume in some places and raise it in others. For instance, you might want the intro music to fade out as you begin to talk. **To make volume changes to *sections of a track,*** GarageBand contains a hidden track called the *volume curve.* See the following page for details.

Use the volume curve

To show the volume curve, click the Show Curves button in the track's header (shown below). A "curve track" appears directly beneath the selected track, with a pop-up menu in the header that shows the default selection of "Track Volume."

To create control points (small blue or green orbs) in the volume curve so you can adjust it, click in several places on the horizontal line of the curve.

To increase or decrease the volume at certain points in the timeline, drag the points up or down.

To alter the duration of a volume change between two points (make it slowly fade in or out or make an abrupt change) drag a point left or right.

To delete a point on the curve, click once on it to select it (the orb gets bigger when selected), then hit the Delete key.

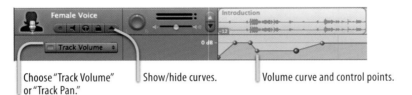

Choose "Track Volume" or "Track Pan."   Show/hide curves.   Volume curve and control points.

To adjust the pan settings of specific sections of the track, choose "Track Pan" from this pop-up menu.

Mix your Podcast

After you finish the basic editing of your podcast (delete unwanted audio, rearrange regions, add additional audio clips, etc.), you're ready for the *mixing* phase of production in which you add jingles, sound effects, and sound filters. Add web links and visuals to create what is known as an **enhanced podcast.**

Loop Browser button.

Loop Browser.

Show podcast sounds.

Drag a jingle from the Loop Browser to the Jingles track.

Add sounds to the "Jingles" track

Your podcast will sound more professional if you include a jingle or theme music. GarageBand automatically includes a "Jingles" track in the podcast project. All you have to do is drag the music you want from the Loop Browser to the Jingles track.

1 First, show the Loop Browser: Click the Loop Browser button (the eyeball icon).

2 Display the podcast sounds: Click the podcast button located in the bottom-left corner.

3 In the "Loops" column, select a category such as "Jingles."

4 In the next column, choose a sub-category, such as "Cinematic."

5 In the next column, select a sound file. **To hear a preview,** single-click any selection.

6 When you find a jingle you like, drag it to the "Jingles" track. Drag it to a position in the timeline where you want it to start playing.

To repeat a jingle, hover the pointer over the *top* half of the region's right edge until it turns into a *Loop pointer* (shown below). With this pointer, press-and-drag the edge to the right.

Blue vs. green loops and tracks

You can drag sound loops from any of the other categories in the Loop Browser to the Jingles track. However, notice that tracks and sound files in the Loop Browser are **color-coded blue and green.**

> **Blue** indicates **Real Instrument** loops and tracks. Real Instruments are actual audio recordings of voices or real musical instruments that were captured by a microphone. You recorded a Real Instrument track in Chapter 5.

> **Green** indicates **Software Instrument** loops and tracks. Software Instruments are digital MIDI files. They're created with a MIDI keyboard or other software instrument. They are more editable than Real Instruments, but they require more computer processing power.

You can only drag blue loops to blue tracks and green loops to green tracks.

For instance, look at the track called "Radio Sounds." When you select it, you can see that it's a green track. If you try to drag a blue loop into it, it won't go. There are a few green loops in the "Sound Effects" category of podcast sounds, but most podcast sounds provided by GarageBand are blue (Real Instruments).

You're not limited to using only loops from the podcast sounds in your podcast. To browse other loops provided by GarageBand, click one of the other buttons—the text columns view or the musical buttons view.

Musical buttons view.

Columns view.   Podcast sounds view.

Find a loop you want to use, then drag it to an appropriate track (blue or green, depending on the color of the loop you chose).

Make new tracks

Instead of dragging a loop to one of the existing GarageBand tracks ("Jingles" or "Radio Sounds"), you can create new tracks.

To create a new track, click the Plus button beneath the tracks. A sheet slides down from the title bar, asking you to choose the type of track you want to create—Software Instrument or Real Instrument. Remember, Real Instruments (blue loops and tracks) require less processing power. This could be a factor depending on the Mac you use, how fast it is, and how much memory is installed; more importantly, a Real Instrument track is for recording your voice.

Use the ducking feature

In GarageBand, you can designate certain tracks to be **lead tracks.** You can designate others to be **backing tracks.** When any *lead track* is playing, the **ducking** feature automatically lowers the volume of any *backing track* (the volume on all other tracks stays the same).

Ducking saves you the trouble of using a volume curve (see page 78) to manually lower the volume of a jingle or sound effect on another track when something more important—such as the narrator's voice—needs to be heard.

If the Mixer column isn't visible, see page 77.

If the ducking controls aren't visible in the Mixer column, go to the Control menu across the top of your screen and choose "Ducking."

These are the ducking controls.

To designate a track as a lead track, click the *top half* of the ducking control (in the Mixer column of the track header). The upward-facing triangle highlights in a gold color.

To designate a track as a backing track, click the *bottom half* of the ducking control. The downward-facing triangle highlights in a blue color.

Combine ducking and manual volume control

Sometimes you will use both ducking and manual volume control. In the example below, the "Jingles" track is designated as a backing track—the bottom half of the ducking control is highlighted.

Its volume will automatically be lowered in deference to any lead tracks playing audio at the same time. In the example below, the ducking feature will lower the jingle's volume, but then it will stop abruptly at the end of the jingle region. We want the jingle to fade out slowly, so we click the Show Curves button to show the volume curve track, then click on the horizontal volume line in two different places to create two new control points (small blue or green orbs, as explained on page 78). We then drag the second point to the right and down to the bottom of the curve track to gradually mute the jingle. The sloped line shows the gradual decrease in volume.

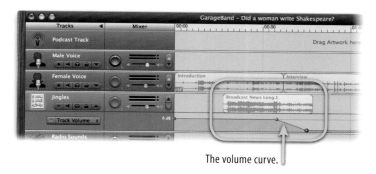

The volume curve.

6 : Edit & Mix your Podcast

Add sound effect filters to a track

GarageBand provides many "instrument" effects that you can apply to a track. They're all fascinating and fun to experiment with, especially to those of us who are new to podcasting and sound production. But use them sparingly in your podcast. Like anything else, overdoing it can be very annoying.

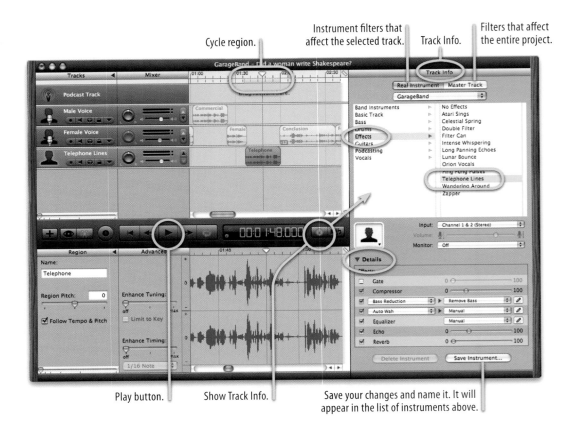

Cycle region.

Instrument filters that affect the selected track.

Track Info.

Filters that affect the entire project.

Play button.

Show Track Info.

Save your changes and name it. It will appear in the list of instruments above.

If you see a photo or "No Artwork Available" in the upper-right space instead of the instruments, click the Details triangle at the very bottom of the pane.

General directions

In the example, you see a region named "Telephone" that was recorded at the same time as the other clips; you might want to add a filter called "Telephone Lines" so it will sound like a telephone interview.

Instrument filters apply to entire tracks, not just selected regions, so if you don't want to apply the filter to the entire track, you first need to isolate the region on its own track: Simply create a new track (see page 82) and drag the region you want to affect to the new track so it's all by itself. Then:

1 Double-click an empty space in the track header to show the "Track Info" pane on the right.

2 In the left column of the Track Info, select "Effects," for instance, then choose an option from the right column.

3 Click the Play button to preview the sound. (This is an example of when it's useful to use the *cycle region* feature explained on page 66.)

4 If you're feeling brave, experiment with the effects on the bottom half of the pane, in the "Details" section (click the "Details" triangle if you don't see these options). Adjust these settings to experiment with effects. You will be asked to save and name the changes you have made; this new collection of customized settings you just created is then available in the list of instruments so you can use it again.

Reduce ambient noise with Speech Enhancer

When you listen to your recording, the ambient noise in the room—or the sound of the computer's fan—may be more noticeable than you thought it would be. To reduce some of that ambient noise, try the "Speech Enhancer" effect:

1 Double-click the track header that contains the noisy audio. This opens the Track Info pane and also selects all of the regions in the track.

2 In the "Details" area of the pane, click the pencil icon that appears to the right of the "Speech Enhancer" pop-up menu (if that first menu doesn't say "Speech Enhancer," choose it).

3 In the new window that opens, adjust the "Reduce Noise" slider to remove as much noise as possible without affecting the audio quality. Play the audio to test the setting.

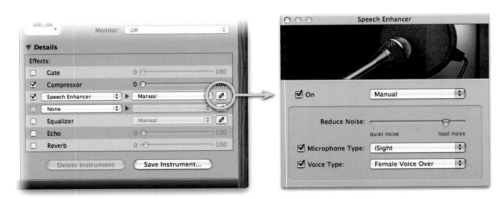

Even out the sound with the Compressor effect

During the creation of a podcast, you may record various audio clips at different times and in different environments, perhaps even using different microphones. As a result, it may be difficult to adjust all of the different audio clips so the volume sounds even throughout the podcast.

In that case, use the "Compressor" effect to even out the volume throughout an entire track.

1 Double-click the track header you want to compress. This opens the Track Info pane and also selects all of the regions in the track.

2 In the "Details" area of the pane, click the Compressor checkbox (if it isn't already).

3 Drag the Compressor slider to the right to even out the volume (play the track to determine how much compression to add).

Experiment with the other instruments and effects!

Musical typing

To add some fun sounds to your podcast, use the "Radio Sounds" track that GarageBand provides in your podcast project. Notice when you click on this track, it's green (the others are blue or purple), indicating that it uses green loops—Software Instrument loops; MIDI instruments attached to the computer; or the onscreen, virtual MIDI keyboard that GarageBand provides (shown below).

If you're not a musician, the virtual keyboard may seem useless to you— but wait—you can "map" all sorts of sound effects to the virtual keyboard and add them to your podcast by clicking keys.

Instrument categories.

Instruments.

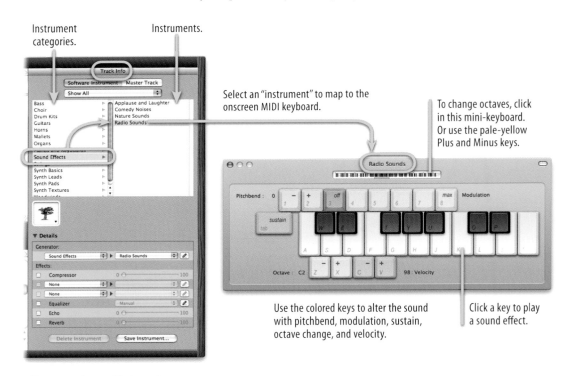

Select an "instrument" to map to the onscreen MIDI keyboard.

To change octaves, click in this mini-keyboard. Or use the pale-yellow Plus and Minus keys.

Use the colored keys to alter the sound with pitchbend, modulation, sustain, octave change, and velocity.

Click a key to play a sound effect.

If you see a photo or "No Artwork Available" in the upper-right space instead of the instruments, click the Details triangle at the very bottom of the pane.

As you select different categories and instruments, the selected track changes its name to match. It is optimized for that particular sound.

To map these sounds to the keyboard:

1 Double-click the "Radio Sounds" track header.

2 From the Window menu, choose "Musical Typing" to open the keyboard window.

3 Choose an "instrument category" on the left side of the upper pane, and then an "instrument" from the right side. **Tap** or **press** the keys on the screen **or** on the corresponding keys on your computer's keyboard. Experiment!

Now, to add these sounds to the green track:

1 Position the Playhead in the timeline where you want to add a sound effect.

2 Make sure the red Enable Recording button is selected in the green track.

3 Click the round red Record button.

4 Tap the keys in the Musical Typing window or on your keyboard.

5 When finished, click the Play button to stop the recording and to stop the Playhead.

6 Close the Musical Typing window to disable it.

Add Artwork to your Podcast

It's not necessary to add graphics to your podcast, but it can make an episode richer, more enjoyable, and even more informative.

When someone plays your podcast in iTunes, the graphics appear in the album artwork pane in the bottom-left corner of the iTunes window. When you publish a podcast to an iWeb page, the artwork is shown right on the web page. Anyone who downloads this podcast to a video iPod will also be able to see the images.

To resize and crop the images in the podcast, see page 98.

iWeb automatically creates a movie player for you. See Chapter 7.

Graphic formats to use for artwork

The most common formats to use for artwork are JPG and PNG. But GarageBand also accepts TIFF, PICT, GIF, BMP, and PSD (Photoshop) file formats.

The optimal size for artwork is 300 x 300 pixels, with a resolution of 72 ppi (pixels per inch). If your artwork is oversized, GarageBand will optimize it to the correct podcast size.

Track graphics and episode graphics

There are two places in the GarageBand podcast project where you can add graphics:

> **The Podcast Track:** This is the top track in the list of tracks (it's purple when you click on it, indicating it doesn't want any music or voice in it). A graphic placed in the Podcast Track displays when the Playhead reaches the artwork's position in the timeline. See page 92.

Podcast Track.

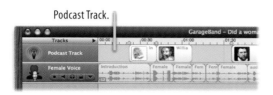

> **The Episode Artwork well:** The well (an empty space waiting for a graphic) is visible in the Track Editor (bottom-left of the window) when you select the Podcast Track and open the Track Editor. Episode artwork displays whenever artwork is not present in the Podcast Track timeline shown above. See page 93 for details.

Episode Artwork.

Add artwork to the Podcast Track

You're going to drag graphics or photos (now called **markers**) from the Media Browser **or** from any location on your computer into the Podcast Track.

1 Click the Podcast Track to select it.

2 If you want to use the Media Browser, click its button (circled below) to show it on the right side. Then click the "Photos" tab in the Media Browser to show iPhoto's contents.

3 Drag an image from the Media Browser **or** from any location on your hard disk and drop it into the desired position in the Podcast Track— a point in the timeline where you want the image to be displayed.

Drag the *image marker* (press in the middle of it) left or right to adjust its exact position in the timeline.

Drag either *edge* of an image marker left or right to alter its duration (how long it's displayed).

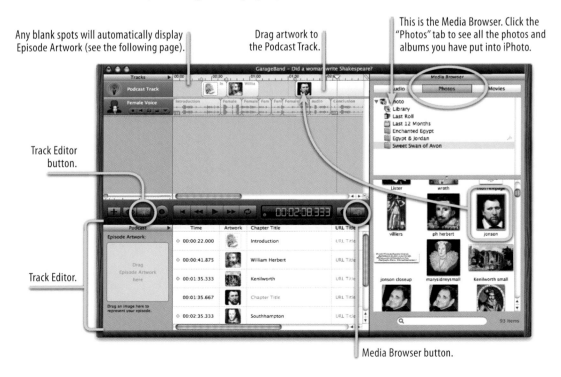

Any blank spots will automatically display Episode Artwork (see the following page).

Drag artwork to the Podcast Track.

This is the Media Browser. Click the "Photos" tab to see all the photos and albums you have put into iPhoto.

Track Editor button.

Track Editor.

Media Browser button.

Add episode artwork to the podcast

You're going to drag graphics or photos (now called **markers**) from the Media Browser **or** from any location on your computer into the Episode Artwork well, as shown below-left.

Episode artwork is a graphic or photo that *represents* the episode. This image (or marker) is displayed in the podcast in iTunes or on the iWeb page whenever you left a blank spot in the Podcast Track.

1   If the Track Editor isn't visible, click the Track Editor button.

2   If you want to use the Media Browser, click its button (circled below) to show it on the right side. Then click the "Photos" tab in the Media Browser to show iPhoto's contents.

3   Drag an image from the Media Browser **or** from any location on your hard disk and drop it into the Episode Artwork well.

These blank spots automatically display the Episode Artwork.

Media Browser button.

Track Editor button.

Track Editor.

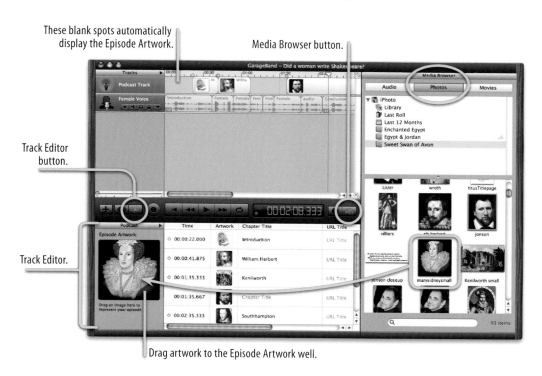

Drag artwork to the Episode Artwork well.

Create Episode Chapters and Chapter Markers

You can define "chapters" in your podcast so listeners on your iWeb page can navigate directly to specific, predetermined sections of the podcast—a very nice feature for podcasts that are long or that contain a variety of topics.

In the movie player on the iWeb page, listeners will be able to select the episode chapter they want to hear from a pop-up menu in the movie control bar, as shown below. Don't worry—you don't have to build any of that. You just set the markers (as explained on the following page) and GarageBand and iWeb do all the rest.

Chapter markers.

Chapter markers appear in GarageBand's timeline as small, gold diamonds.

Create chapter markers, if you like
There are two ways to create chapter markers.

Method One:

1 Drag artwork from the Media Browser **or** from anywhere on your hard disk to the Podcast Track and position it where you want it to appear (as explained on the previous pages).

2 Make sure the Track Editor is showing (if not, click the Track Editor button). The artwork in the Podcast Track is automatically added to a list of *markers* in the Track Editor, shown below.

3 In the list, single-click the default name ("Chapter Title") and *type a new name* for the marker. Hit Return or Enter. **Doing this creates a chapter marker** (a gold diamond) in the timeline.

This new title will appear in the player's pop-up menu of episode chapters on the web page (shown on the opposite page).

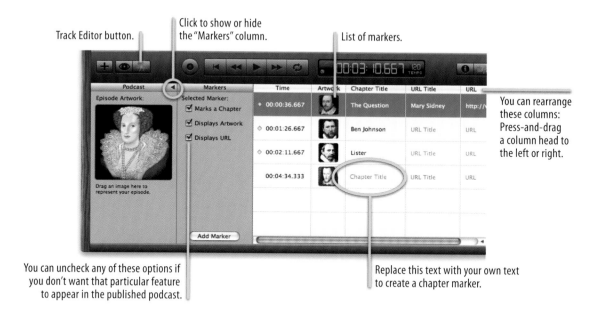

Track Editor button.

Click to show or hide the "Markers" column.

List of markers.

You can rearrange these columns: Press-and-drag a column head to the left or right.

You can uncheck any of these options if you don't want that particular feature to appear in the published podcast.

Replace this text with your own text to create a chapter marker.

Method Two:

1 Position the Playhead in the timeline where you want to create a chapter marker.

2 Click the "Add Marker" button in the "Markers" column of the Track Editor (if the "Markers" column isn't visible, click the small triangle in the heading of the "Podcast" column).

3 When you create a chapter marker this way, it's blank—episode artwork will display while this chapter plays. **To add an image to a blank chapter marker,** drag an image from the Media Browser (or from anywhere on your computer) to the marker's image well in the Artwork column, as shown below.

4 Single-click "Chapter Title" to rename it.

The Playhead's position in the timeline.

This new chapter marker doesn't have an image associated with it.

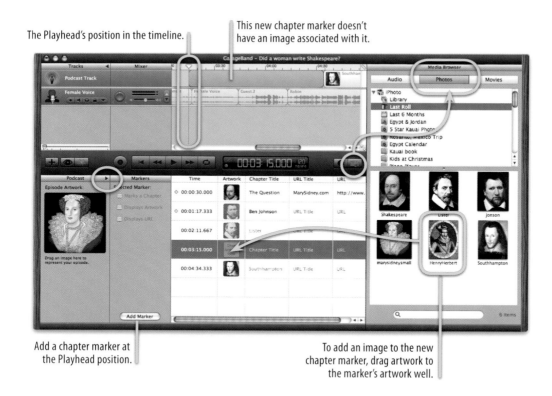

Add a chapter marker at the Playhead position.

To add an image to the new chapter marker, drag artwork to the marker's artwork well.

Add a URL to an image in the podcast

You can add a web address (URL) to any chapter marker. If the image displays long enough during the podcast, the listener can click on it. A new web page will open to that address, and the podcast will continue playing.

1 Select a chapter marker in the list.

2 In the "URL Title" column, single-click on the default text "URL Title" and type a *description* of the web site. This name will appear in light gray until you enter the URL in the next column.

3 In the "URL" column, single-click on the word "URL" and type the web address you want to display; hit Enter or Return. You don't need to type http:// because GarageBand will fill that in for you automatically.

4 Click the Info button to display the artwork, as shown below. Click the link on the artwork to check it.

Click the Track Info button to
show the "Podcast Preview" pane.

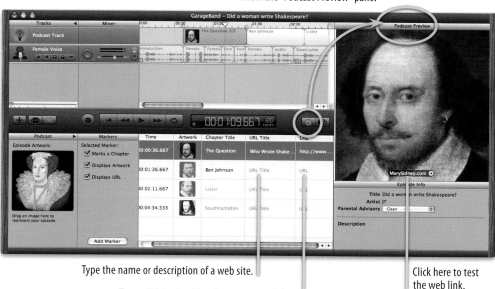

Type the name or description of a web site.

Type a URL (web address) you want to link to.

Click here to test
the web link.

Size and Crop Podcast Photos

You can resize and crop the images you add to your podcast.

1 Double-click the image in the Episode Artwork well, **or** double-click one of the photos in the "Artwork" column of the markers list.

2 In the "Artwork Editor" that opens (shown below), drag the slider to resize the image.

3 Press-and-drag the image inside the frame to change the cropping.

4 Click the "Set" button to apply your changes.

Preview your Podcast!

You will probably want to preview your podcast all along the way.

1 Open the Track Info pane by clicking on the Track Info button, the little **i**, as shown on the previous page. Or just double-click the Podcast Track header.

2 In the player controls, click the left-facing single triangle (shown on page 64) to send the Playhead all the way to the beginning.

If you want to preview your podcast from another starting point, just click in the tic marks at the very top of the timeline to make the Playhead jump to that position. Or drag the Playhead manually to where you want to start the preview.

3 Click the triangular Play button to start and stop the preview. It will display in the big top portion of the Track Info pane on the right.

Add Episode Info

The Episode Info pane adds information about your podcast that will be visible when it's viewed in iTunes. It's also visible on your podcast page in iWeb.

1 Double-click the Podcast Track header. The right side of the GarageBand window reveals the "Podcast Preview" pane and the "Episode Info" pane.

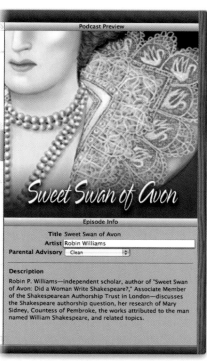

The image displayed in the Podcast Preview pane is determined by the current position of the Playhead in the timeline. To add episode information, it doesn't matter what image is currently displayed or where the Playhead is.

2 The "Title" field contains the name of your GarageBand project. To change it to something else, click on the existing title and type a new one.

3 Click "Artist" to enter your name or the name of a featured guest in the podcast.

4 From the "Parental Advisory" pop-up menu, choose a description of the podcast— None, Clean, or Explicit.

5 Click the "Description" field to type a description of your podcast series or of this specific episode.

Share your Podcast

After you've recorded, edited, and mixed your podcast project in GarageBand, you can share it in several ways. The Share menu shows your options.

Send Podcast to iTunes

This command creates a *mixdown* of your project, converts it to a format that's compatible with iTunes (AAC audio file), and puts it in *your* iTunes— in the playlist you created in GarageBand preferences (see page 54). This is for your own personal use; no other iTunes user will see it. See Chapter 8 for details about how to get your podcast series listed in the iTunes Directory for the world to subscribe to.

Send Podcast to iWeb

This is the option you'll use to post your podcast to your iWeb site (even if you don't have one yet). Details are in the following chapter.

Export Podcast to Disk

This command will create a copy of your entire podcast project on a disk that you insert, either for backup or to share. If the Podcast Track isn't visible (from the Track menu, choose "Show Podcast Track"), only the audio part of your project will be exported.

Add your Podcast to the iWeb Site

Your podcast is recorded, edited, and mixed, and you're ready to put it on a web page so you can upload it!

The basic process is incredibly simple: In GarageBand, go to the Share menu and "Send Podcast to iWeb."

But there are a few caveats, depending on whether you've already built an iWeb site and what pages you have already created. So it will behoove you to read on a bit.

Send your Podcast to iWeb

Your podcast is finished. Now you can put it on an iWeb page and share it with the world.

If this is your first iWeb site, carry on with Step 1.

If you have an iWeb site started and it includes a "Blog" page, add a "Podcast" page before you send your podcast from GarageBand to iWeb. If you don't, your podcast will automatically be placed on your "Blog" page (which is actually okay, if you don't mind).

If you have an iWeb site started and it includes a Podcast page (but not a Blog page), your podcast will automatically be placed on the podcast "Entries" page.

If you have more than one site in iWeb and they both have "Blog" or "Podcast" pages, you will be asked which one you want to post this podcast to. It's a good idea to give the multiple "Blog" and "Podcast" pages different names so you can tell them apart.

To send a podcast from GarageBand to iWeb:

1 Open GarageBand and make sure your podcast project is visible in the window.

2 From GarageBand's Share menu, choose "Send Podcast to iWeb."

3 GarageBand converts the podcast project to the proper format and opens iWeb for you.

4 If you don't have a "Blog" or "Podcast" page in iWeb yet, you'll be asked to select a theme from the left-hand pane, then a "Blog" or "Podcast" page from the right (podcasts can be placed on either one). Later you may choose to include both types of pages in your site, but for now choose the "Podcast" template, then click "Choose."

If this is the first time you have opened iWeb, it creates a web site (named "Site" in the "Site Organizer" pane) that consists of three pages: "Podcast," "Entries," and "Archive." Carry on through this chapter to edit your pages. Be sure to add a Welcome page before you publish (see Chapter 2 for details on adding and editing pages).

If you have an existing site to which you are adding this page, you will now have the Podcast set of pages as described above and on the following pages.

Edit your Podcast

An "Entries" page opens in the iWeb window and shows the podcast that you sent from GarageBand.

To preview your podcast, click the Play button on the player's control bar. Replace, edit, and customize the text and graphics just as you learned in Chapter 2.

Double-click to customize the placeholder page heading. The date appears automatically.

This placeholder title also appears in the list of entries at the top of the window. Change it on the page and it will also change in the list above.

Or double-click the title in the list above, make changes, and it will change the page heading.

The description you typed in GarageBand is included with the podcast that you sent to iWeb from GarageBand. You can edit it here.

The Podcast Set of Pages

When you add a podcast, iWeb actually adds a *set* of three pages—**Blog, Entries,** and **Archive**—as you can see in the Site Organizer. Each of these pages has a very important function. We'll explain each of these pages separately. Click the page link in the Site Organizer to show the page.

The "Podcast" page

This is the page your visitors will see on your site once it's posted to the web. You can edit everything on this page *except* the podcast text itself, the piece you see circled in the graphic below. You can't edit this because iWeb automatically generates this from your Entries, as shown on the next page. You can resize this text block or move it, but don't delete it!

To publish your site so you can check it out while you're working on it, just click the "Publish" button at the bottom-left of the iWeb window and it will publish to your .Mac account. For details, see Chapter 8.

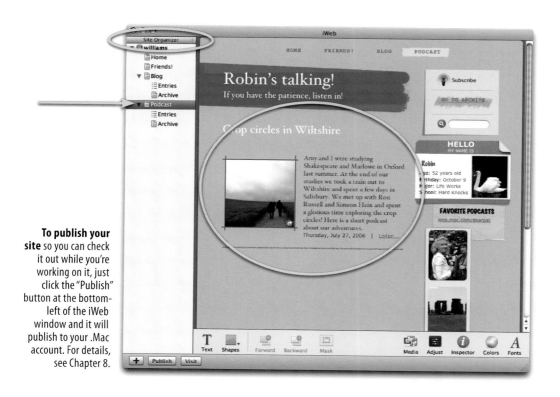

The "Entries" page

This is where you will manage your podcasts. Whenever you send a new podcast to iWeb from GarageBand, it lands on this *Entries* page. Edit the text and graphics, if you like, then publish.

> **Make a new entry:** Click the button "Add Entry," then replace the existing text and graphics. Sending a podcast from GarageBand is not the only way to add podcast: You can drag a podcast from the Media Browser or anywhere on your Mac and drop it into the placeholder graphic. (If you drop it anywhere else on the page, people will be able to listen to it, but not subscribe to it.)

> **Delete an entry:** Select an entry name in the top list of entries, then click the "Delete Entry" button.

> **Change the date:** You can pre- or postdate your entries by double-clicking on the date in the upper-right column. Change the date, then click anywhere on the iWeb page to set it.

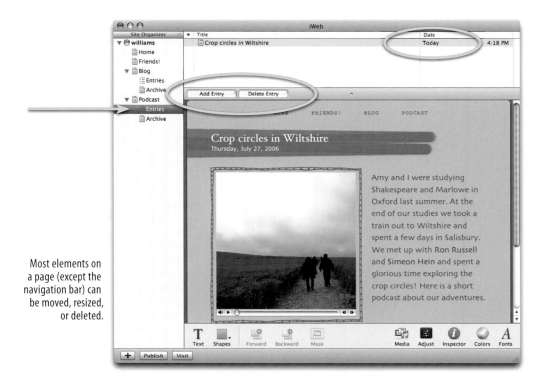

Most elements on a page (except the navigation bar) can be moved, resized, or deleted.

The "Archive" page

iWeb updates this page for you whenever you add a new podcast. You can't do anything to this page except change the title, rearrange items, and delete the Subscribe button or search field. iWeb automatically generates this page and the text, based on the information on your Entries page.

When visitors to your podcast click the "Go to Archive" button on your podcast page, it takes them to this *Archive* page where iWeb has created linked excerpts of your descriptions of each podcast.

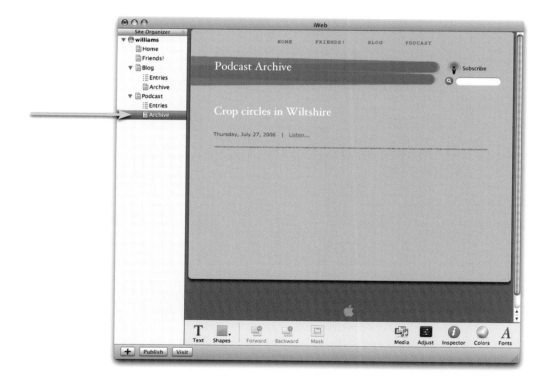

All Done?

Once you've added the podcast and edited your text and designed the site pages, you're ready to publish your iWeb site and begin your podcasting empire. A typical, ready-to-publish site is shown below. Your site will look different, of course, depending on the template you chose and the content you created. You can click the "Publish" button at the bottom-left of the iWeb window to publish the site to your .Mac account, or see Chapter 8 for details before you click.

This is the existing podcasting entry shown in the window below.

The page icons' red color indicates that the current changes have not yet been published.

When you add a new podcast from GarageBand, iWeb automatically makes a new entry page for you.

Or click "Add Entry" and drag a podcast from the Media Browser or anywhere on your hard disk and drop it in the placeholder movie.

The new podcast is automatically added to the list of podcasts on the main "Podcast" page.

Publish your Blog & Podcast

Most of the work is done! Once your site is up, all you'll do is regularly update it and add additional podcasting episodes and blog entries. It will be a matter of typing your blog entry or creating a podcast and hitting the "Publish" button. Woo hoo!

A .Mac Account?

The easiest way to publish your iWeb site, as we've mentioned before, is to have a .Mac account. If you have one (and only one), skip this page—go to the next page and publish!

If you have more than one .Mac account

Your iWeb site will be published to the .Mac account that is active on your Mac at the moment you click the "Publish" button. The active account is the one currently shown in the .Mac system preferences, as shown to the right (go to the Apple menu and choose "System Preferences…," then click the ".Mac" icon). If you want to publish to a different account, enter its name and password here, then publish.

If you don't have a .Mac account, this button says "Learn More." If you'd like an account, click this to go straight to the sign-up page on Apple's web site.

If you don't have a .Mac account

You can publish your site to a folder on your Mac and tell iWeb to post it on the server of your choice. See pages 125–126.

If you want to buy a .Mac account (it comes with lots of great features), go to Mac.com and sign up for one. Or open your .Mac system preferences, as explained above, and click the "Learn More" button—it takes you to the .Mac web page on Apple's site. The $99/year price is a bargain for all the fun and functionality that a membership offers. There are Family Packs available also, for up to five people.

Publish your iWeb Site

You have probably already published your site by now, but here are details just in case! Remember, if you have more than one .Mac account, see the previous page before you publish. And if you don't have a .Mac account, skip this page; see pages 125–126.

Publish to your .Mac account

Click the "Publish" button in the bottom-left corner of the iWeb window.

Your published site will have an address of **http://web.mac.com/YourSiteName**.

The first time you publish your site, all of the pages and hundreds of secret files (containing lots of code you didn't have to write and lots of images you didn't have to create) are published, so it can take several minutes. After the first upload, iWeb will only publish pages that have changes on them so it will be a lot faster.

You might get a warning message about making sure you are not uploading copyrighted material without the proper permissions.

Your .Mac account password was automatically entered in Keychain (an application that keeps track of your passwords). You'll see an alert box to "Confirm Access to Keychain." Click "Always Allow" or "Allow Once." If you share your computer with other users, it's safer to choose "Allow Once."

—continued

iWeb starts uploading your site to your .Mac account. A sheet slides down to tell you that the publishing process will continue in the background. Click OK.

This icon shows the publishing progress.

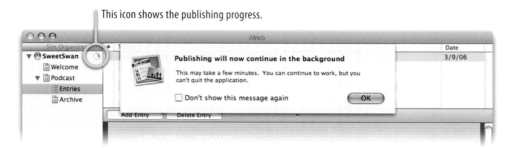

Once the site is published, another sheet slides down to alert you. You're done! Go check out your site on the web!

Your site's web address is shown here. Because you created a Welcome page, it's an easy address to remember.

Choose to "Announce" your site to others (iWeb will help you send email), "Visit Site Now," or click "OK" and return to iWeb.

A Few Tips

Here are a couple of extra tips about publishing your iWeb site to your .Mac account.

Republish the entire site

Sometimes you might want to completely republish an entire site instead of just pages that have changes. If so, in iWeb go to the File menu and choose "Publish All to .Mac."

Reload or refresh the page

Whenever you republish your site or a page, you might not see the changes on the web right away. If your browser has been to that page before, it puts a copy of it in your "cache" so when you ask for it again, it doesn't have to go back to the web and get it—it grabs it from the cache on your hard disk. So when you make and upload changes to a page, you might not see them because your browser is showing you the cached page.

To tell your browser to go back to the server and get the new page, find and choose the menu command in your browser called Reload or Refresh (it's usually in the View menu).

If you still don't see the changes, your browser might think it's smarter than you—it might have gone back to the server and decided there were no changes. **To force it to reload the page,** hold down the Shift or the Option key and choose the menu command again (different browsers use different keys).

Submit your Podcast to iTunes

You can submit your brilliant podcast to the iTunes Music Store for all the world to see and hear (and subscribe to). Humans at Apple review your podcast submission and can choose to reject it if it's found unsavory for some reason, so keep that in mind.

When you submit your podcast, you assign keywords and categories that make it easy for others to find your podcast when they search iTunes.

While people can always listen and subscribe to your podcast by visiting your web site, submitting it to iTunes adds another way to make it accessible, especially for those who might not find your site. And it's free.

You need either a .Mac account (you can get a free trial and after the trial period is up, keep the screen name), an AOL account, or a free AIM account (sign up for one at AIM.com).

1 Open iWeb.

2 In the Site Organizer, select the main "Podcast" page to submit the whole series, or on the "Entries" page, select just a single entry (episode).

3 Open the Inspector (click the "Inspector" icon in the toolbar on the bottom-right of the iWeb window). In the Inspector, shown on the opposite page, click the "Blog & Podcast" button (RSS), then click the "Podcast" tab.

If you entered an "Artist" name in GarageBand in the Podcast Preview info window, it will appear here.

4 Enter information about the podcast series (if you're submitting several podcasts) or episode (if you're submitting a single podcast).

Series Artist: Name the artist, author, or featured guest.

Parental Advisory: assign a category of "Clean" or "Explicit" to alert parents about the nature of the podcast content. Or choose "None."

Contact Email: This provides a way for iTunes to contact you (your email address won't appear in iTunes).

Allow Podcast in iTunes Music Store. Make sure this item is checked.

5 From the File menu, choose "Submit Podcast to iTunes."

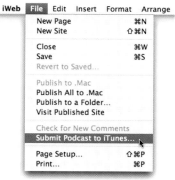

—continued

6 In the sheet that drops down, as shown below, enter information about your podcast. Some of it might be filled in already.

Drag an image and drop it in this spot. This will appear in iTunes. Make sure you own the copyright to the image.

The **description** in the purple area is the description you wrote in iWeb on the "Podcast" page, right below the title. In iTunes, part of this description will appear in the "Description" column to the right of the podcast name; when someone clicks the small Info button in that column, a "Podcast Information" window opens to display the full text of your description.

To change the artwork that represents your podcast, drag an image on top of the graphic placeholder or the existing image.

7 Click the "Publish and Submit" button. iTunes opens and connects to the Music Store so you can finish the submission.

8 The text field (shown below) automatically contains the URL for your podcast. Click "Continue."

9 Apple requires that you sign in to the iTunes Music Store with your Apple ID and password. This will be your .Mac account name and password (or click the "AOL" button and use your AOL screen name or your AIM name and password). Click "Continue."

10 A "Review Podcast" page opens in the iTunes window. Check to make sure the information is correct, then click "Submit."

This is the title that you entered on your main Podcast page.

This is where the name will appear that you entered in the "Series Artist" field of the Podcast Inspector (see page 115).

—continued

11 The submission of your podcast is complete and the iTunes window displays a "Thank You" message. Click "Done."

Apple sends an email to notify you that your podcast is under review. Podcasts are reviewed and approved by real people, so it takes several days before they show up in the iTunes Music Store.

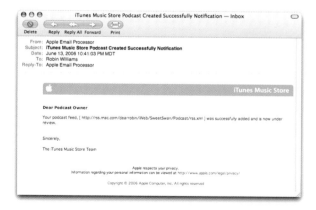

Remove a podcast from iTunes

You can remove an entire series or individual episodes from the iTunes Music Store. Be aware that it takes several days for it to disappear.

1 In iWeb, if you want to remove the entire series from the iTunes Music Store, select the main "Podcast" page.

If you want to remove an individual podcast, go to the "Entries" page and select the individual entry from the list at the top.

2 Open the Podcast Inspector, as shown below.

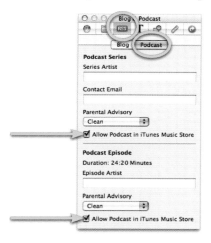

3 Uncheck the box to "Allow Podcast in iTunes Music Store" for either the series (the top half) or the individual episode (the bottom half).

4 Republish the site.

RSS: What is It?

You often hear the term "RSS feeds" when people are talking about blogs and podcasts. RSS stands for **Really Simple Syndication.** It's a technology that enables others to subscribe to your blog or podcast.

Subscribe to a blog

iWeb's *blog* templates include an **RSS Subscribe** button. People who use RSS readers can click that button to have the feed directed to their reader.

Safari, installed on your Mac, is an RSS reader. **To get an RSS feed** of any blog using Safari:

1 When a page has an RSS feed, Safari displays the blue "RSS" icon in the location bar, as shown circled below.

2 Click that "RSS" in the location bar **or** click the "RSS Subscribe" button on the blog page. This opens the RSS feed, as shown on the opposite page.

3 On this page you will see all the recent articles that have been published by this person. On the right-hand side of the browser window, you have many options for organizing this information. Experiment with the options.

4 To have these articles "fed" to you, first make sure your "Bookmarks Bar" is showing, as shown below (if it isn't, from the View menu choose "Show Bookmarks Bar").

5 Make a bookmark of this page, rename it with a short name that you'll remember, and save it into the Bookmarks Bar, as shown below.

This is the new RSS bookmark in the Bookmarks Bar. Now when Robin's mom posts a new blog, the number of unread blogs will appear in parentheses.

6 Whenever that person posts a new blog, you will see a number in parentheses in your Bookmarks Bar. That's your clue to click on that bookmark to read the new posts.

You don't have to save an RSS feed in the Bookmarks Bar—saving the bookmark into your bookmark menu will work just as well, but you'll have to pull down your menu to see if any new blogs have been posted.

Subscribe to a podcast

iWeb's *podcast* templates include a **Podcast Subscribe** button. There are a variety of podcast players, software or hardware, that play the recording for you.

iTunes is a podcast player, of course. **To subscribe to a podcast** using your Mac and iTunes:

 Subscribe **1** On a podcast page, click the "Subscribe" button or the "RSS" in the location bar.

2 iTunes opens and loads the podcast, as shown on the opposite page.

3 Because you are now subscribed to this podcast, you can always find it in iTunes—just click the "Podcasts" item in the Source pane to display it.

When the podcaster adds a new podcast, it will display here in iTunes. You can always force it to go check and update by clicking the "Update" button in the upper-right corner of the iTunes window.

Note: *Keep in mind that when you place a podcast episode on your iWeb page by dragging it from the Media Browser or from any location on your computer (as opposed to sending it to iWeb through GarageBand), you must drop the podcast in the podcast placeholder on the page. If you drop it in any other location on the page, it will **play**, but visitors won't be able to **subscribe** to it.*

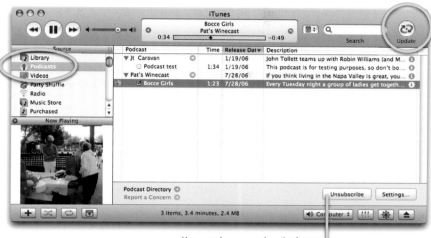

You can always unsubscribe from a
podcast: Select it, then click this button.

Customize your podcast subscription settings

In the iTunes preferences, shown below, click the "Podcast" icon so you
can choose how often you want iTunes to check for new episodes of
subscribed podcasts. When new episodes are found, they're downloaded
to iTunes and placed in the "Podcasts" playlist, circled above.

Bandwidth Issues

When a visitor plays your podcast, a certain amount of bandwidth (data transfer) is used. Providers who host podcasts have data transfer limits for how much bandwidth your account is allowed over a certain period of time. If your podcast becomes hugely successful, the bandwidth you use could possibly exceed the allotted amount and your provider could charge you for the extra bandwidth used. It's not likely this will be a problem for casual podcasters. If your podcast does get that popular, you can probably get advertisers to sponsor your podcast and cover the cost—plus make a profit.

When you use .Mac to host your podcast and reach your data transfer limit, you (or your visitors) will see a message that you've reached your limit.

A basic .Mac membership provides 1 GB of storage and 10 GB (gigabytes) of data transfer per month. You're allowed to use up to half of your allotted amount during the first fifteen days of the month. If you exceed your limit, your site is turned off until the beginning of the next monitoring period (the 1st or 16th of the month, whichever comes first).

Increase your allotted amount of bandwidth (up to 250 GB/month) by buying more .Mac storage space; you can get up to 4 GB for an additional $99.95/year. Log in to your .Mac account to buy more, or use the Site Inspector in iWeb.

A rough estimate of bandwidth useage for a podcast is approximately 0.5 MB/min (megabytes per minute) for audio-only podcast files. Podcasts with visuals or video average around 1–2 MB/min.

Some third-party podcast hosts offer flat fees with unlimited storage space and unlimited bandwidth.

Publish to other Places

You can publish your iWeb site to a server other than .Mac, or to your .Mac HomePage or Group page, as explained on the following pages.

Publish to another server

If you have an existing web site that's not a .Mac site, you may want to publish your new pages there.

To upload to a server other than .Mac, you first must publish the site to a folder *on your computer*. Then you'll upload that folder to the server where you have your main web site.

1 Open iWeb. In the Site Organizer, select the site that you want to publish to another server.

2 From the File menu, choose "Publish to a Folder...."

3 In the sheet that slides down, choose a location on your computer in which to store your site.

4 Click the "New Folder" button to create a folder for the site. Name it with your iWeb site name ("SweetSwan" in this example). This folder name will become part of the web address, so don't use spaces.

5 In the URL text field shown below, enter the URL for the site where you are going to upload your iWeb site. After the site name, type a slash, then the folder name you just created. The URL should look something like this: **http://www.YourWebSite.com/FolderName/**

iWeb uses this address to create the code necessary to turn your blogs and podcasts into "RSS feeds" so others can subscribe to them.

6 Click "Choose." —continued

7 A sheet slides down with the options to "Visit Site Now" (the site will open from its folder location on your computer), or click "ok" to return to iWeb.

As the sheet above points out, certain iWeb features are supported only if published to a .Mac account: enhanced slideshows, the hit counter, password protection, blog search field, and the ability to let others add comments and attachments to blog pages.

Now it's your responsibility to upload that folder you just created to your web site server.

Keep in mind that this site will not be automatically updated when you click the "Publish" button in iWeb!

After uploading the folder we made, the SweetSwan site (and its blog and podcast) is accessible on the MarySidney.com site at **http://www. marysidney.com/SweetSwan**.

Publish to HomePage

A .Mac membership includes a feature called HomePage for creating web sites online. If you would like to add your iWeb site to your already existing collection of HomePage sites, you can.

Since you've already created a web site in iWeb, all you have to do is publish your iWeb site to a folder on your Mac, then upload that folder to the "Sites" folder on your iDisk (the storage space on Apple's servers that comes with a .Mac membership).

1 Open iWeb. In the "Site Organizer" pane, select the site you want to publish.

2 From the File menu, choose "Publish to a Folder…" (see pages 125–126, Steps 2–7, for instructions).

3 Put that new folder on your Desktop for now.

4 Now open your iDisk: Go to the Finder. From the Go menu, choose "iDisk," then choose "My iDisk."

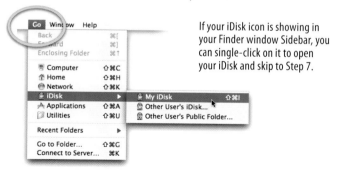

If your iDisk icon is showing in your Finder window Sidebar, you can single-click on it to open your iDisk and skip to Step 7.

5 An icon for your iDisk appears on your Desktop (it's a blue crystal ball).

roadrat

—continued

6 Double-click the iDisk icon to open your iDisk in a window, as shown below.

7 Drag the folder you created in Step 2 into the "Sites" folder found in your iDisk.

Your site's URL will be: **homepage.mac.com/MemberName/FolderName**.

In this example, we copied a folder named "SweetSwan" to John's "roadrat" "Sites" folder, so the address is: **homepage.mac.com/roadrat/SweetSwan**.

Publish to a .Mac Group page

Another cool feature of .Mac membership is the Group web page. Only people whom you have invited and approved are allowed access. You can enable Group members to add comments, photos, blogs, podcasts, etc. It's a great way to keep members of a group in touch with each other—classmates, teammates, friends, relatives, co-workers, or any other group.

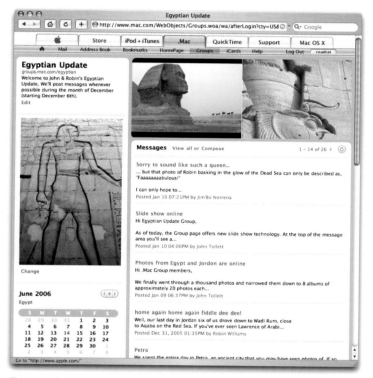

This is a typical Group page. There are too many wonderful features about a Group page to mention here! Go to Mac.com and read all about it.

—continued

If you're a member of a Group page—and if the Group administrator has granted permission—you can add your podcast to the Group page.

1 In the Site Organizer in iWeb, select the site whose podcasts you want to add to a Group page. Every page in your site will be accessible, although only the podcasts will be listed on the Group home page.

2 In the Site Inspector (shown to the right), check "Publish to a group," then select a Group's name from the pop-up menu (all Groups to which you belong will appear in this menu).

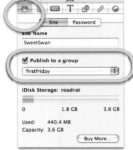

3 In the iWeb window, click the "Publish" button. The items in the Site Organizer turn blue.

4 Go to your Group page (**http://groups.mac. com/GroupName**), then look for the podcast in the left column, in a section called "Our Pages."

Carry On!

So now you should feel comfortable creating new blogs and podcasts and publishing them to your iWeb site. Oh, you will be the talk of the town.

If you want to be the talk of the Internet, you're going to have to do a lot of promoting! We give you some tips on this in the next chapter.

Tell the World About your Blog or Podcast

If your blog or podcast is a personal one for family or friends, or perhaps an internal company podcast for employees, you may not need to publicize it—just send an email to the intended audience that includes the URL (web address) for the site. Or publish an announcement on the family web site or in your company newsletter. If you've created a private family Group page, you can publish your blog/podcast site there and post an announcement that it's available (see pages 129–130).

But if your podcast and/or blog is public, you'll probably want the world to know. How many listeners or subscribers you reach depends not only on promotional efforts, but also on the information or entertainment value of your content. And of course, to build an audience of subscribers, you need to provide new episodes on a regular basis.

Most podcasters and bloggers want as large an audience as possible. Really marketing your own site can be a part-time job in itself. If you're serious about it, search the web for "promote your podcast" or "promote your blog." You'll be amazed at the results of your search. What we hope to provide in this chapter is a number of suggestions that will *help* in your promotion.

Promote your Podcast

There are a few things you can do while creating your podcast that will help people discover it later, plus here are a few ideas for ongoing promotion.

Describe your podcast

During the process of producing your podcast in GarageBand and iWeb, you have several opportunities to write a description of it (as in the pane shown below). When writing these descriptions, be as concise yet descriptive as possible. Use as many keywords as you can in the description that relate to the podcast. When you submit your podcast to a directory (see pages 19, 93, and 97), an accurate description helps others decide if they want to listen to an episode or subscribe to your podcast.

When a GarageBand, iWeb, or iTunes dialog box requests information, don't leave those fields blank! All of the requested information is helpful when someone is searching for your podcast.

Use your most important keywords here!

Podcast directories

A podcast directory collects the web addresses and descriptions of published podcasts that have been submitted to them. People search the directories for podcasts that interest them by entering podcast category terms or topic keywords in the directory's search field. For someone to find your podcast and listen to it, you need to submit it to as many directories as possible—simply go to the directory and click their button that says something like "Submit" or "Add your Podcast."

When you submit a podcast to a directory, you're asked for the RSS feed URL. This is the web address where your podcast is published. When iWeb published your site (containing a podcast) to your .Mac iDisk, it created an RSS Feed URL in this format:

Popular directories

There are many online podcast directories that will list your podcast for free. Search the web for "podcast directory." Some of the most popular:

PodcastAlley.com   Podcast.net
PodcastPickle.com   PodcastingNews.com
Odeo.com   Podcasts.Yahoo.com/publish

There are many more, but one that's unique is Podzinger.com. Podzinger uses speech-to-text technology to make the podcast's audio searchable. The Podzinger search results show snippets of text that highlight the search terms used. When you click on a highlighted word in a snippet, the audio plays from that point in the podcast. Try it.

—continued

The iTunes podcast directory

iWeb provides an automated process for submitting a published podcast to iTunes, as explained on pages 114–117. Once you're listed in the iTunes directory, anyone can search there for your podcasts.

Like any directory, the iTunes Music Store doesn't actually *publish* podcasts—the directory just lists podcasts and points to the web addresses where they're published.

iWeb works with iTunes to automate the process of submitting a podcast to the iTunes podcast directory.

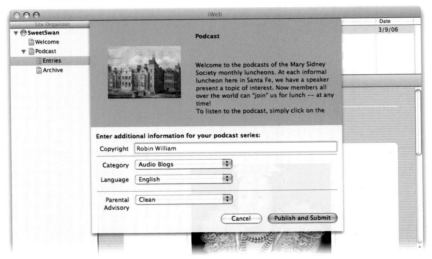

Promote your Blog

Also, we highly recommend you search Guy Kawasaki's blog for articles about promoting your blog. He's in the top 100 most-read blogs, so he should know how to make it happen!

blog.GuyKawasaki.com

There are many types of blogs—news, educational, training, personal, etc. Each type may, to some degree, require a custom approach to promotion and publicity. Even so, most all blogs benefit from some basic techniques of promotion.

Apple provides a promotional opportunity as soon as you publish: When your site is successfully online, iWeb gives you a message that your site is now posted and includes an "Announce" link. Click "Announce" and an email form opens with a brief message and a link to your iWeb site. Address the email to your address book list, modify the message in whatever way you like, then send the announcement.

One very important recommendation: Make sure you include an "RSS Subscribe" button on your blog page. iWeb automatically puts one on the page for you—you can move it, but don't delete it. It lets the site visitor easily subscribe to your blog or podcast.

If you care about building an audience, one of the most important things you can do is submit your blog address to as many directories and blog search sites as possible. There are hundreds to choose from. You'll find a long list of directories at rss-specifications.com. Just a few of the popular sites for submitting blogs are Technorati.com, Feedster.com, BlogSearch. Google.com, Yahoo.com, and Bloglines.com. Pingomatic.com will alert a variety of directories that your blog has been updated, making it easier for people to find you and, in the process, making your site more likely to be picked up by the appropriate directories.

When you visit other blogs that have a comments feature, leave a comment (a nice one). Most of these allow you to leave a signature and a link (to your blog). Visitors read the comments left on bloggers sites, so if your comment is worthy, other visitors might also go to your site.

Some search engines and directories put more value on sites that have incoming links. Try to get other sites to link to your blog.

When you give out contact information, include your blog address— on email signatures, business cards, brochures, ads, and all other promotional materials.

There is an abundance of information online about how to publicize your site, and if you're serious about getting your blog well known, you will need to spend some time learning the latest tricks. Do a search for "promote your blog."

Cross-Promote your Blog and Podcast

Cross-promote your blog and podcast by advertising the name and web address everywhere you have a presence—in a newsletter or self-promotion brochure, on other web sites, in print advertising, during radio interviews, etc.

Put a "signature" in your email that includes the web address, so every email you send is a promotional piece. (To create one or more signatures for yourself in Apple's Mail application, open the Mail preferences and use the "Signature" pane.)

If you know other podcasters, get an interview or have them mention your podcast on their show. Trade links with other bloggers.

Even without a budget, you can increase the size of your audience through word-of-mouth. Tell others about your podcast and blog, and include your iWeb information on your business cards.

If your blog or podcast is for an organization, cross-promote it through channels already available to the organization.

If it's press-worthy, send a press release to the local media announcing the launch.

Try an on-site podcast: Go to a small café or a special area to record your podcast ("Live from the historic Plaza in downtown Santa Fe"). Interview people and pass out cards that include your podcast name and address.

It's not necessary to have ambitions for a national audience, or even a regional one. You might just want to reach family, friends, associates, or neighbors. In this case you can limit your promotional and publicity efforts to small efforts that are appropriate. For instance, if your potential audience is your own retirement community, place a notice on the community bulletin board or in the monthly newsletter. The grown kids and grandkids might want to know how much fun you're having, so pass along the web address to them in an email or announce it on a family web site (such as a Group site you can create with your .Mac account).

Once you've started a podcast, try to publish new episodes on a regular basis. It's easier to build an audience if your schedule is frequent and reliable.

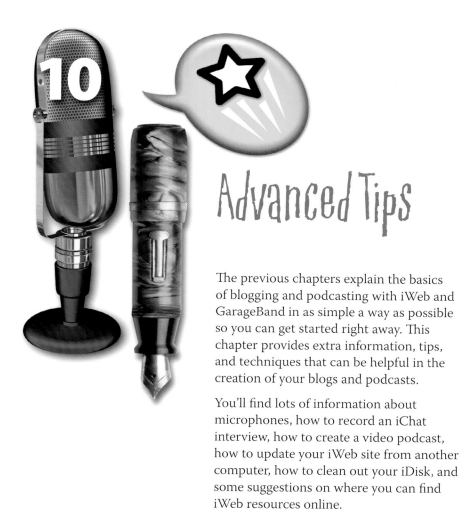

Advanced Tips

The previous chapters explain the basics of blogging and podcasting with iWeb and GarageBand in as simple a way as possible so you can get started right away. This chapter provides extra information, tips, and techniques that can be helpful in the creation of your blogs and podcasts.

You'll find lots of information about microphones, how to record an iChat interview, how to create a video podcast, how to update your iWeb site from another computer, how to clean out your iDisk, and some suggestions on where you can find iWeb resources online.

Do You Need a Microphone?

Creating a blog is relatively simple—just type your message, then publish it to your .Mac account using iWeb. Even though GarageBand and iWeb make podcasting easy, there's no denying that it's a bit more complicated than blogging. One of the complications is in deciding which microphone to use for recording your podcast audio.

Using your computer's built-in mic (if it has one) is fine for learning how to podcast, and it usually works great for personal and family podcasts, for a podcast directed to a group of friends, or a small organization. But if you hope to build a large audience, you'll soon want to consider other microphone options.

Ordinarily, the built-in mic on a laptop does a pretty good job of recording voices. But too often, the hard drive and fan create a background noise that's very noticeable on the recorded audio. It's hard to eliminate this problem completely if you have a noisy computer, but using an external microphone can help the situation by moving the microphone and person who's speaking further away from the source of the noise.

Another way to eliminate computer noise is to record your voice using the built-in mic of a digital video camera (in a quiet room), then import the audio into GarageBand (as explained on page 144).

While learning all about microphones is a career path all its own, the following pages will give you a brief overview of the most common types of mics, some popular mics to consider, and a little bit about audio interfaces (hardware that connects between your computer and your microphone).

External microphones

The two basic types of external microphones you'll choose from are **condenser** mics and **dynamic** mics.

Condenser microphones use technology that makes it possible to create miniature mics, such as lapel mics and the built-in mics found in computers (condenser mics can also be full-sized). They require a power supply, such as an internal battery; or they can draw power from an input port (such as a USB port) to which the mic is connected; or through *phantom power* (drawing the power from a connected device such as an *audio interface*—see page 145 or 149). You might hear this type of condenser mic called an *electret* mic.

Condenser mics are more sensitive than dynamic microphones. They also have a more limited sound input level, beyond which the sound output will be distorted (called clipping). This type of mic also generates a certain amount of electrical noise that can possibly be heard as a hissing sound in the background, especially with less exensive models. GarageBand's built-in filters can help to minimize this effect when it happens.

Dynamic microphones use a different technology that prohibits miniaturization, so this type of mic isn't used for computer built-in mics or lapel mics. Dynamic mics are tougher, more durable, and don't need an external power supply as required by condenser mics. And, unlike condenser mics, they can handle the loudest sound levels without distortion—which makes them a popular choice for stage performers.

Microphone connection types

Some external microphones plug straight into your computer by way of the USB, FireWire, or analog audio-input port (a ⅛" mini jack).

This is the analog audio-input port on a PowerBook.

Other microphones use connectors that cannot connect directly to your computer—a ¼" jack or an XLR connector. If you want to use one of these mics you need a special box called an *audio interface* (sometimes called a *breakout box*) that plugs in-between your microphone and your computer (see pages 145 and 149).

USB

Microphones with a USB connector can plug straight into your computer. They're available in a wide range of prices.

FireWire

The Apple iSight camera contains a built-in microphone and connects via FireWire. It's the only FireWire microphone available.

Mini phone plug
(also known as the ⅛" or 3.5 mm plug)

This ⅛ connector is used on many different microphones. It plugs into a computer's audio input port or into an audio interface that provides a mini jack plug, such as the Griffin iMic.

You can plug a mic that uses a mini jack into a ¼" phone plug adapter (shown below), then plug the adapter into a ¼" phone jack (such as the ¼" phone jack ports found on many audio interfaces).

The number of rings on a phone plug identifies it as a stereo (two rings) or mono (one ring) plug.

Why are they called phone jack connectors? They get their name from ancient times when this connector was used on telephone switchboards.

¼" phone plug
(also known as the 6.3 mm plug)

This is another common type of connector for microphones (similar to the ones shown above). Macs don't have ¼" phone jacks, so you need to use an audio interface to use mics with this kind of connection.

XLR

Many professional microphones use this type of connector. To get audio from an XLR microphone to your computer requires an audio interface, or you can buy an XLR adapter that connects via mini-jack to the audio-in port of your computer (shown at the bottom of the page).

This type of microphone connector was originally developed by a company named Cannon. The microphones that used it were called the *Cannon X* series. Subsequent versions added a latch (*Cannon XL*) and later a rubber compound was added around the connector contacts (*Cannon XLR*). Today, any microphone that has this type of connector is referred to as an XLR mic.

XLR connectors (male and female).

This XLR adapter combines an XLR connector and a mini-jack connector.

Microphone suggestions

If you're planning to do regular podcasts that are a notch above beginner level, we recommend buying a consumer-level microphone at first to keep things simple and affordable. The following items are mics we've used, but there are lots of other great choices. Look online for microphones from companies like M-Audio, Sennheiser, Behringer, and Shure. Or visit your favorite music or electronics store—some of them may let you try different microphones in the store.

Logitech USB desktop microphone

This small, portable microphone plugs straight into your computer's USB port and costs less than $30. The sound quality is superior to most built-in mics and it's an affordable way to start your podcasting empire. Logitech.com

Samson Co1U condenser microphone

This high quality microphone connects directly to your computer's USB port. It costs around $80. SamsonTech.com

Behringer studio condenser microphone C-1

A high quality mic that uses an XLR connector. It's very affordable at approximately $50, but you'll need an audio interface to connect it. Behringer.com

Sony ECM-MS907 electret condenser microphone

This small microphone has outstanding quality and sensitivity, uses a ⅛" stereo mini plug, and gets power from a AA battery. You can connect it to the Griffin iMic audio interface (page 145), then plug the iMic into your computer's USB port. You can find this mic online for around $70.

iSight camera

An external Apple iSight camera includes a microphone. It connects to your computer with a FireWire cable. The $149 price tag is fairly expensive for just a consumer microphone, but the inclusion of video capability makes the iSight a good value.

The built-in audio quality of the newer iMacs and laptops that provide *built-in* iSight cameras seems to be better than that of the built-in microphones in older (PowerPC) laptops and iMacs. Apple.com/store

Lavalier microphones

A lavalier microphone (also called a lapel mic) can be used to record your podcast. Lavaliers are small, inexpensive, and they allow the presenter to have some freedom of movement—if the lavalier cable is long enough. Lavalier microphones usually have a mini-jack connector and aren't self-powered, so you'll need an adapter that plugs in-between the lavalier and your computer.

This is a Griffin lavalier microphone connected via mini phone plug to the In port of a Griffin iMic USB audio interface.

In this case, we like to use a miniature USB audio interface made by Griffin called iMic. We plug a lavalier's mini jack into the IN port of the iMic, slide the iMic's input slider to MIC, then connect the iMic to our computer's USB port. Now when we select our audio input in GarageBand preferences (see page 55), the Audio Input pop-up menu includes the option of "iMic USB audio system." And, of course, this technique works with other microphones besides lavaliers.

Wireless microphones

You could possibly have a recording situation in which a wireless microphone is needed. For example, perhaps you want to record a presentation and the presenter's style is to walk all around the stage, into the audience, back to the podium, etc.

Wireless microphones have two basic parts: a transmitter worn by the person whose voice you want to record, and a receiver that connects to your computer (or some other recording device).

We occasionally use the Samson AL1 Lavalier System. Its transmitter includes a tiny built-in microphone, or you can connect it to a lavalier mic.

As with lavalier microphones, you need a device that interfaces between the wireless receiver and your computer. Once again, the iMic is designed to do just that. Plug the iMic into a USB port on your Mac, then plug the wireless receiver into the "IN" jack on the iMic. In GarageBand preferences, from the Audio Input pop-up menu, choose "iMic USB audio system."

The Samson transmitter with built-in mic is worn by the presenter.

The Samson receiver connects to your computer (or video camera).

Use a digital video camera as a microphone

Another way to get audio for your podcast into GarageBand is to record your voice onto a Mini DV tape using a FireWire-enabled digital video camera. You can then connect the video camera to your Mac and import the footage into iMovie HD (the movie editing software included in iLife '06). iMovie can move the audio part of the recording into iTunes, where GarageBand's Media Browser can access it.

There are several reasons why you might want to do this. You may prefer the sound quality provided by your video camera, especially if your only other option is the computer's built-in microphone. Or you may want to record an interview or a narrative at a time or place in which your computer isn't available or where it would be inconvenient or awkward to use. And finally, you might want to capture video so you can have the option of creating a video podcast.

To transfer audio from your camera to GarageBand:

1 Put a Mini DV tape in your video camera. Make sure the camera is in "Record" or "Camera" mode. Press the Record button and speak into the microphone. Press the camera's Record button again to stop recording. Now rewind the tape in the camera.

2 Use a FireWire cable to connect the video camera to your Mac.

3 Open iMovie and create a "New Project."

To select iMovie's Camera mode (for importing video), click the camera icon.

4 Make sure the camera is in Play or VCR mode.
   Make sure iMovie is in Camera mode.

5 Click the "Import" button in iMovie's preview window to import the podcast footage and sound from the tape in your camera.

6 Select the imported clip in iMovie's Clips pane (you don't have to drag it to the iMovie timeline). From iMovie's Share menu, choose "GarageBand." Check the box that says "Share selected clips only," then click the "Share" button. This opens GarageBand and places the *selected* clip into a "Video Track" and a "Video Sound" track.

7 Select the Video Sound track and copy it (Command C) so you can paste it into an existing or new GarageBand podcast project. You don't have to save the iMovie project—just quit iMovie.

8 Open or create a podcast episode in GarageBand, then select an audio track (or create a new audio track) and paste the iMovie audio into the selected track.

Audio interface

If you buy a microphone that doesn't connect to a USB port or audio-in port on your computer, you'll need a device called an **audio interface.**

An audio interface is a box that contains input and output connectors, plus controls for adjusting and monitoring audio that you record. Most importantly, an audio interface provides connectors that don't exist on your computer, such as XLR and ¼" jacks. Using an audio interface is one way to record with more than one mic at a time. Some audio interfaces provide just a couple of microphone or instrument plugs, others let you connect many different types of mics and instruments at once.

A large variety of audio interfaces are available—both USB and FireWire models—made by companies such as Edirol.com, M-Audio.com, and Tascam.com. Look for them online, in music stores, or electronics stores. A simple, inexpensive (but limited) audio interface is the Griffin iMic (shown below-left).

A term you'll see associated with audio interfaces and condenser microphones is **phantom power.** This is a method of providing required power to a condenser mic through its cable. It's called phantom power because it's invisible to mics that don't need it. For instance, you could have both a condenser mic and a dynamic mic connected to an audio interface at the same time. Audio interfaces provide an on/off switch for phantom power because some older types of mics can be damaged by it.

When you connect a USB condenser microphone directly to your computer, power for the mic is supplied from the computer through the USB cable.

The Griffin USB iMic costs about $30.

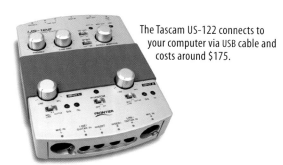

The Tascam US-122 connects to your computer via USB cable and costs around $175.

10 : Advanced Tips

Other recording tips

Microphones are sensitive instruments and they sometimes pick up or exaggerate sounds and noise that you don't even notice until you hear it on the recording. To minimize such problems, you can invest in some inexpensive noise filtering devices for your microphone.

Pop filters and wind-screen filters

Speaking into a microphone often creates a popping sound when you pronounce consonants, especially Ps and Bs. A pop filter (also known as a P-pop filter) is a small screen placed in front of a mic to eliminate that effect.

A wind-screen filter is usually made of foam and slips over the head of a microphone like a sleeve to minimize the sound of wind hitting an unprotected microphone grill. If a wind screen from your video camera microphone fits over your podcasting mic, it can also serve as a pretty good pop filter.

This shows a wind-screen filter slipped over the head of a Sony ECM-MS907 electret condenser microphone.

A typical pop filter attached to a microphone stand.

Sound-condition your recording environment

Unless you're recording on location and don't have any control over the recording environment, try to record in a quiet room that muffles sound—drapes on the windows, carpet on the floor, etc. A podcasting friend of ours put carpet on the walls of a small, unused room and turned it into his podcasting studio. The less sound that bounces around in the recording area, the better your recording will sound.

Practice with your microphone

If the mic you decide to use is new to you, record some practice clips with it to determine the distance from the mic that works best. You should also experiment with the input volume setting in your Sound preferences (page 57) to discover how different settings affect your mic.

Headphones are useful

A good set of studio-style headphones will give you the truest representation of what your audio really sounds like as you record, edit, mix, and review. Studio headphones have big puffy pads that cover your ears and block out much of the ambient noise in a room, like the hum of your computer's fan and processor. (Headphones also provide a pleasant and quiet environment for other people nearby, especially when you're editing and mixing.)

Microphone summary

It can be very frustrating trying to decide which microphone to use because there are so many options available. It doesn't take long to realize that the world of audio is huge, complex, and very technical.

Beginning podcasters should keep it simple and inexpensive. A built-in microphone is good enough to learn podcasting. If you want to upgrade to an external mic, a $30 to $50 mic will satisfy most non-professionals. Remember, entertaining or informative content is more important to your audience than Hollywood-quality audio.

Podcasting with Multiple Microphones

Podcasting with one microphone in GarageBand, a built-in mic or a plugged-in external mic, works well enough in most instances, but you may encounter situations in which having two or more microphones is better. For instance, if your podcast involves an interview of someone, it's more comfortable and the sound quality is better if you each have your own mic. And there could be editing advantages to having each voice on a separate audio track.

Connect multiple mics to your computer

To set up GarageBand so each connected microphone records on a separate track:

1 Connect the microphones to your computer.

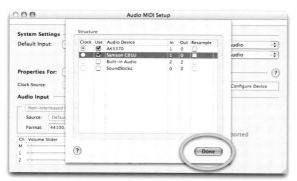

2 From the Utilities folder (inside the Applications folder), open Audio MIDI Setup. From the Audio menu, choose "Open Aggregate Device Editor." Connected audio devices (mics) are listed in the sheet that drops down (shown to the left). Checkmark the devices you want to activate, then click "Done."

3 Open GarageBand preferences, then open the "Audio/MIDI" pane. Make sure the "Audio Input" pop-up menu selection is "Aggregate Device."

4 Open the Sound pane of System Preferences, then click the "Input" tab. In the list of sound input devices, select "Aggregate Device."

5 In GarageBand, double-click an audio track (such as the default "Male Voice") to show the "Track Info" pane. From the "Input" pop-up menu, choose "Channel 1 (Mono)." Now select a second audio track (such as the default "Female Voice") and from the "Input" pop-up menu choose "Channel 2 (Mono)."

GarageBand is now set up to record each mic on a separate audio track.

Connect multiple mics to an audio interface

Another way to use multiple microphones is to connect an audio interface between the computer and the mics. The USB Tascam US-122, shown below, connects to the computer's USB port for power, and a mini-jack cable connects the Tascam to the computer's Audio-in port ().

To use GarageBand with an audio interface:

1 Connect an audio interface to your computer, then connect the microphones to the audio interface.

Mini-jack connection to computer's Audio-in port.

USB connection to computer.

XLR dynamic microphone

XLR dynamic microphone

2 Open GarageBand preferences and click the "Audio/MIDI" button in the toolbar. From the "Audio Input" pop-up menu, select the name of the connected audio interface.

3 Open the Sound pane of System Preferences, then click the "Input" tab. In the list of sound input devices, select the name of the connected audio interface.

4 Open Audio MIDI Setup (found in the Utilities folder, which is inside the Applications folder). From the "Default Input" pop-up menu, select the connected audio interface.

—continued

5 In GarageBand, double-click an audio track (such as the default "Male Voice") to show the "Track Info" pane. From the "Input" pop-up menu, choose "Channel 1 (Mono)." Now select a second audio track (such as the default "Female Voice") and from the "Input" pop-up menu choose "Channel 2 (Mono)."

Now GarageBand is set up to record each individual microphone's input on separate audio tracks.

Record an iChat Interview

iChat and GarageBand can work together to create a podcast interview with someone who's in another location—even on the other side of the planet. Even though your iChat might be video, GarageBand will not record the video—it will take snapshots, however, each time a different person starts to talk!

To record an iChat in GarageBand:

1 Open GarageBand and choose "New Podcast Episode." Name the episode and save it.

2 Open iChat and double-click the person in your Buddy list whom you want to interview.

3 Start your audio or video chat.

4 When you're ready to start recording into GarageBand, click the Record button in the GarageBand window.

5 An alert window opens to ask if you want to record the active iChat conference that GarageBand has detected. Click "Yes."

6 GarageBand automatically creates a new track for each conference participant and begins recording each voice in its own track.

If the iChat conference is a video chat, GarageBand captures a still photo (from the live video) each time it detects audio in a participant's audio track. It places the photos in the Podcast Track (the top track).

7 To stop recording, click the Record button again.

Add any editing and mixing you want, just as you would with any podcast project. You can choose to replace the automatically captured photos with other photos or graphics.

GarageBand automatically puts a single-frame video capture in the Podcast Track when a participant speaks.

GarageBand creates a new track for each iChat participant.

What's a Video Podcast?

A video podcast is basically a standard audio podcast with video added. Because video files are much larger than audio files, they'll take up a lot more room on your iDisk (assuming you're using your .Mac account and the easy-to-use integration of .Mac publishing and iWeb). If you have a digital video camera and iMovie, you can be a video podcaster.

The best way to create a video podcast is to first create a movie version of your podcast presentation in iMovie. iMovie lets you can add transitions, titles, slides, filters, and special effects. When you're happy with the edited version, you can send the movie project from iMovie to GarageBand or straight to iWeb.

There are some advantages to routing the movie through GarageBand: You might plan to create an original music score in GarageBand; you can add some of the audio filters and special effects that GarageBand provides; GarageBand provides a "Description" field to inform listeners about the podcast's content; you can add additional audio tracks to record voice-over narration or interviews to go with the existing video.

This is a video project as it appears in iMovie.

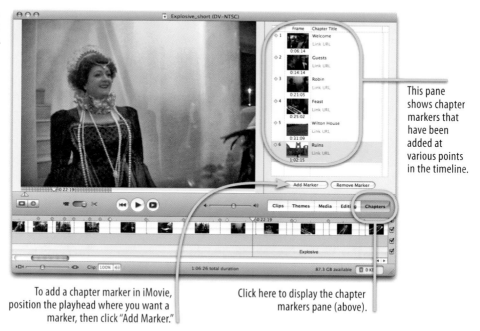

This pane shows chapter markers that have been added at various points in the timeline.

To add a chapter marker in iMovie, position the playhead where you want a marker, then click "Add Marker."

Click here to display the chapter markers pane (above).

Create a video podcast

Here are the guidelines to make a video podcast, using iMovie, GarageBand, and iWeb:

1 Create and edit a video presentation in iMovie.

2 **To include chapter markers,** click the "Chapters" button, position the playhead where you want to place a marker, then click "Add Marker" (see the previous page). Name the marker something relevant. If you choose not to include chapter markers at this stage, you can add them later in GarageBand.

3 From iMovie's Share menu, choose "GarageBand." GarageBand opens and automatically creates two new tracks: A "Video Track" that contains the iMovie video, and a "Video Sound" track (shown below).

To display the GarageBand window as shown here, with the "Video Preview" and the "Video Markers" panes visible, click the Track Editor button (the scissors icon, circled), then double-click the "Video Track" at the top of the window.

This is a movie project in GarageBand.　　　Playhead.　　　Video Preview.

Two new tracks.

Track Editor button.

Add a marker.

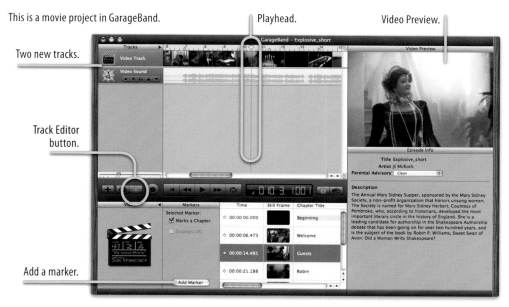

—continued

4 GarageBand sees the markers that you created in iMovie and shows them in the Markers pane. Click on the chapter marker names in the lower middle section and change them if you want.

To add new chapter markers, drag the playhead to a point in the timeline where you want to place a marker, then click the "Add Marker" button in the "Markers" pane.

5 When you're satisfied with the podcast, go to the Share menu and choose "Send podcast to iWeb."

6 If a "Podcast" page doesn't yet exist, iWeb creates one for you, as shown below.

If you already have a "Podcast" page set up in iWeb, the video file is placed there.

If you have a "Blog" page already set up, but not a "Podcast" page, the podcast gets placed on the "Blog" page.

7 Replace the placeholder text on the iWeb page with your own text.

8 When you've made all of your changes, click the "Publish" button in the bottom-left corner.

Drag a video into GarageBand

You can also drag a video file from the Media Browser (or from any location in the Finder) into the top of the GarageBand window. The track (named "Podcast Track") is converted to a "Video Track," and a new "Video Sound" track is added beneath the "Video Track" (as shown on page 153).

You can place only one video file in the Video Track. If you add a second file to the track, it *replaces* the existing video.

If your video is shorter than the podcast duration, the last frame of the video will display to the end of the podcast.

Chapter markers aren't visible in the iWeb window shown on the opposite page. After the site is published, they appear in a pop-up menu on the web page's video player, as shown here. When a viewer chooses one of the chapter names in the list, the video jumps to that point.

Update your iWeb Site from Another Computer

Your iWeb site is completely contained on your Mac in a secret folder away from your prying hands. This means that you can't update it from any other computer except the one you created it on. But perhaps you want to take your show on the road and need to update your site from a laptop. What can you do?

Domain.sites

We'll tell you how to find your secret folder and take it with you. All of the files that make up your site are saved in a single package called "Domain.sites" (the file may appear simply as "Domain"). This is where it's stored:

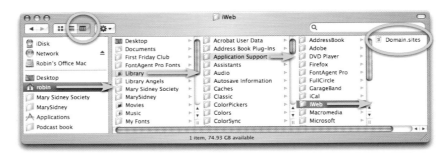

To make a copy of "Domain.sites," quit iWeb, locate the file, then Option-drag it to your Desktop.

When you copy the "Domain.sites" file to another Mac (one that has the same version of iWeb installed), you can store the file anywhere, not just in the Library folder. You can even rename the first part of it so you know it's not the original one (don't change the ".sites" extension).

To work on your site using your copy of the domain file, first quit iWeb, if it's open. Then double-click the "Domain.sites" file that you copied. This makes iWeb open your site just as if you were working at home (or wherever you usually work). iWeb saves all of your changes in the current "Domain.sites" file that you're now working with.

To publish changes from this secondary computer, make sure you've got your .Mac account name in the .Mac preferences, as explained on page 110. (If you're using someone else's computer and you accidentally upload to their .Mac account, this will replace any iWeb site they may have had on the web! Fortunately, they can re-publish theirs to replace it.)

Make a copy of this version of the file when you finish so you can have an updated "Domain.sites" file to replace the older file on your other computer.

If there are several iWeb sites on your computer (several "Domain.sites" files), iWeb will automatically open the one most recently launched when you open iWeb. **To open a different iWeb site** than the last one opened, locate its "Domain.sites" file and double-click it.

Clean Out your iDisk

If you post a number of web sites and delete pages and add more sites and delete sites, you will undoubtedly end up with excess stuff in your iDisk that is taking up space. You can open the Web folder on your iDisk and carefully remove files that you know you don't need.

To open your iDisk, single-click its icon in your Sidebar. On your iDisk is a Web folder, shown below. Use the column view in your window and follow the path to your sites folder. Do not remove any file that you are not absolutely sure you can remove safely!

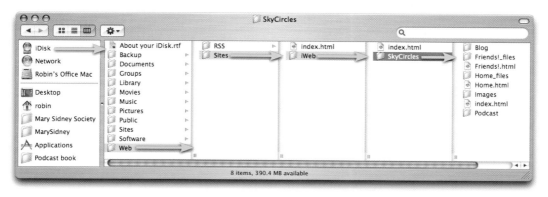

iWeb Resources Online

Even if you love the iWeb template designs, it's always nice to have even more choices. A few designers and third-party developers offer iWeb design templates for reasonable fees. Search the web for "iWeb templates." A couple of the sites you'll find are Lamiavia.com and iLifeStuff.com.

Some designers/programmers are doing amazing things with iWeb, in spite of the built-in limitations that are meant to keep unskilled web designers from totally wrecking the page design and functionality. To find examples of enhanced iWeb design, search the web for "iWeb design."

You can find lots of sites that offer iWeb tips, techniques, and discussions. Try searching for "iWeb tips," "iWeb pages," or something similar.

Of course, you can find iWeb information in its Help file (from the Help menu, choose "iWeb Help" or "iWeb Getting Started"). Or go to Apple.com/support/iweb.

Lamiavia.com

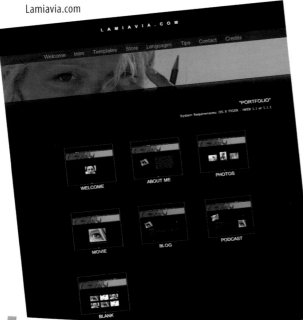

iLifeStuff.com

The Index

Symbols